AIR VANGUARD 7

USAF MCDONNELL DOUGLAS F-4 PHANTOM II

PETER DAVIES

First published in Great Britain in 2013 by Osprey Publishing,
Midland House, West Way, Botley, Oxford, OX2 0PH, UK
43-01 21st Street, Suite 220B, Long Island City, NY 11101, USA
E-mail: info@ospreypublishing.com

Osprey Publishing is part of the Osprey Group

A CIP catalog record for this book is available from the British Library

Print ISBN: 978 1 78096 608 3
PDF e-book ISBN: 978 1 78096 609 0
EPUB e-book ISBN: 978 1 78096 610 6

Index by Mark Swift
Typeset in Deca Sans and Sabon
Originated by PDQ Digital Media Solutions Ltd., Suffolk, UK
Printed in China through Bookbuilders

13 14 15 16 17   10 9 8 7 6 5 4 3 2 1

www.ospreypublishing.com

Osprey Publishing is supporting the Woodland Trust, the UK's leading
woodland conservation charity, by funding the dedication of trees.

GLOSSARY

AAA	antiaircraft artillery
ADC	Air Defense Command
AKG	Aufklarungsgeschwader (reconnaissance wing)
ANG	Air National Guard
BDA	bomb damage assessment
BLC	boundary layer control
BLU	bomb live unit
CADC	central air data computer
CAP	combat air patrol
CBU	cluster bomb unit
CCTW	Combat Crew Training Wing
CONUS	continental US
COSS	computing optical sight system
CRT	cathode ray tube
CTS	command/telemetry system
DEAD	destruction of enemy air defenses
DIAS	digital integrated avionics suite
DMAS	digital modular avionics suite
EADS	European Aeronautic Defence and Space Company
ECM	electronic countermeasures
FFAR	folding-fin aircraft rockets
FIS	fighter interceptor squadron
FS	fighter squadron
HOBOS	homing bomb system
HOTAS	hands-on throttles and stick
HUD	head-up display
ICE	improved combat efficiency
IFF	identification friend or foe
INS	inertial navigation system
IR	infrared (homing)
JaBoG	Jagdbombergeschwader (bomber wing)
JG	Jagdgeschwader (fighter wing)
LCOSS	lead-computing optical sight set
LGB	laser-guided bomb
LORAN	long-range aid to navigation
LOROP	long-range oblique photography
LRU	line-replaceable unit
MBR	multiple bomb rack
MER	multiple ejector rack
MFD	multi-function display
MiGCAP	MiG combat air patrol
NULLO	not under live local operator
PACAF	Pacific Air Forces
PDM	program depot maintenance
PPI	plan position indicator
PUP	performance update program
QRA	quick reaction alert
RAAF	Royal Australian Air Force
RHAW	radar homing and warning system
RoKAF	Republic of Korea Air Force
RTAFB	Royal Thai Air Force Base
SAM	surface-to-air missile
SEAD	suppression of enemy air defenses
SLEP	service life extension program
SOR	Specific Operational Requirement
TEREC	tactical electronic reconnaissance sensor
TAC	Tactical Air Command
TFS	Tactical Fighter Squadron
TFTS	Tactical Fighter Training Squadron
TFW	Tactical Fighter Wing
TTW	Tactical Training Wing
TISEO	target identification system, electro-optical
TRS	Tactical Reconnaissance Squadron
TRW	Tactical Reconnaissance Wing
UHF	ultra-high frequency
USAFE	United States Air Forces in Europe
VPAF	Vietnamese Peoples' Air Force
WSO	weapons system operator

CONTENTS

USAF MCDONNELL DOUGLAS F-4 PHANTOM II

INTRODUCTION

When the first F4H-1 emerged from the McDonnell Aircraft Company's St Louis factory in May 1958 some observers undoubtedly reconsidered the old adage, "if it looks right it will fly right." Its upswept outer wing panels, severely drooped tail-plane and pendulous nose prompted humorists to suggest that the fighter had been rolled out upside down. Conceived as a naval interceptor, its bulky dimensions did not imply fighter-like performance to pilots brought up on nimble dogfighters like the F-86 Sabre. Closer inspection revealed a lack of guns (previously deemed essential for a true fighter) and a second cockpit, very much at odds with the established solo fighter mentality. When those skeptics heard that the aircraft could carry up to 16,000lb of ordnance (roughly the loaded weight of an F-86A Sabre) and nearly 13,000lb of fuel (2,000lb heavier than an empty F-86A), that fighter designation would have seemed more puzzling. However, a glance at the huge, twin jet exhausts would have revealed the fighter's main strength: more raw power than any previous fighter could muster. With more than seven times the thrust of the F-86A, the F4H-1 could take full advantage of its load-carrying performance and turn its apparent disadvantages into war-winning fighter-bomber qualities.

Although the US Air Force had been interested in the F4H-1 from the outset, it was the revelation of the fighter's substantial ordnance-carrying capability that swung a decision to break precedent and order a US Navy-inspired design from a company that had worked mainly to Navy contracts.

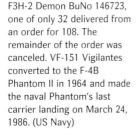

F3H-2 Demon BuNo 146723, one of only 32 delivered from an order for 108. The remainder of the order was canceled. VF-151 Vigilantes converted to the F-4B Phantom II in 1964 and made the naval Phantom's last carrier landing on March 24, 1986. (US Navy)

In October 1945 McDonnell received its first USAF task. Reviving the "parasite fighter" concept, the company designed the XF-85 Goblin, a tiny jet fighter carried beneath Strategic Air Command's mighty B-36 intercontinental bombers for limited air defense over targets. This project was quickly abandoned, but in 1947 the McDonnell design team under Herman D. Barkey produced a far more practical bomber escort, the long-range, twin-jet XF-88. This evolved into the F-101 Voodoo escort fighter by May 1953, and 77 F-101As were ordered. Displaying their customary skill in maximizing the potential of each design, McDonnell adapted the Voodoo to changing USAF demands, giving the F-101A/C nuclear strike capability. Further redesign yielded the RF-101A/C reconnaissance variant, a stalwart performer in Vietnam and numerous Cold War scenarios. Adding a second cockpit, air-to-air missiles and an advanced Hughes MG-13 fire control system in 1956 gave the USAF and Royal Canadian Air Force the F-101B/F and long-serving CF-101B all-weather interceptors.

The Voodoo was large and heavy, 67.5ft long in its RF-101A/C form and weighing up to 52,400lb. It followed McDonnell's well-tried, twin-jet approach to providing enough thrust and an element of safety for over-water operations. The company's only single-engined production fighter, the F3H Demon, had been critically under-powered. When work began in 1945 on the McDonnell's first design, the FH-1 Phantom (the first jet designed for aircraft carrier use), its two jet engines yielded only 1,600lb of thrust each. Sixty were produced and over 850 of a developed version, Barkey's successful F2H Banshee, were delivered to the US Navy and Royal Canadian Navy. Specialized, radar-equipped and reconnaissance variants were included, but performance was still limited by a total thrust of around 7,000lb. Versatile Banshees fought in the Korean War and the aircraft brought considerable profit to McDonnell, remaining in production until 1953, the year in which design work began on the F4H. In its definitive F-4 Phantom versions the resultant aircraft is often judged the greatest jet fighter ever built. Its production run of 5,201 exceeds that of any other modern Western fighter aircraft. It served with 83 wings and groups of the USAF and Air National Guard, 60 units of the US Navy and US Marines, and 11 other nations' air forces. With frequent updates this fighter, which entered operational service in 1961, will still be in front-line use with several air forces up to 55 years later. This partly reflects the aircraft's relatively low initial purchase cost compared to the billions of dollars required to purchase a few of its 21st-century successors, but it is primarily a recognition of the F-4's sheer quality in performance and adaptability. In the skies above Southeast Asia and the Middle East, F-4s flew countless combat sorties delivering a vast range of ordnance against punishing defenses, with reconnaissance data, protection from enemy defenses and fighter escort often being provided by other Phantoms. F-4 crews have claimed victories over more than 350 enemy aircraft in aerial combat since 1965. It is unlikely ever to have an equal.

DESIGN AND DEVELOPMENT

The McDonnell F2H Banshee's immediate successor, the F3H Demon, reversed the company's profitable financial ascent, almost bankrupting it in 1954. The end of the Korean War terminated F2H production – an additional blow. A Navy-sponsored engine competition in 1947 had produced the

The USAF Phantom's immediate predecessor at McDonnell, the F-101 Voodoo, reverted to the company's usual twin-engined layout, adding (for the F-101B interceptor version) a second cockpit for a radar operator, with strengthened undercarriage and bigger tires like the F-4C Phantom. Armament, carried internally, included the Hughes GAR-8 (AIM-4) Falcon, which proved less successful in air-to-air combat for the F-4D/E Phantom. (USAF)

Westinghouse J40, promising 10,500lb of afterburning thrust. It never met that target, and an increase in aircraft weight from 22,000lb to 29,000lb as the Navy switched its role from short-range interception to long-range air superiority seriously reduced the F3H's design performance. It lost a fly-off competition with Chance Vought's F8U Crusader as the Navy's new supersonic day fighter. After several accidents with J40-powered F3H-1s, chief designer Richard Deagan was allowed to replace the J40 with the established Allison J71 (producing 14,250lb of afterburning thrust) for the 459 F3H-2/2M Demons that eventually entered USN service from 1956. Twenty-nine earlier F3H-1Ns, unable to take J71s, were scrapped. Although the Demon remained stubbornly subsonic, it provided experience of the Sperry Sparrow III (AIM-7C) and its associated APG-51A fire control radar, invaluable in developing the F4H-1. It also reinforced McDonnell's belief in twin powerplants.

Despite its disappointing performance, the Demon provided a solid foundation for the F4H. When studies for a new fighter began in McDonnell's advanced-design "cage" at St Louis in 1953, they initially proposed little more than a twin-engined Demon to recoup some of the investment in the stalled F3H program. This proposal, suitably modified, won a September 1954 "letter of intent" for an all-weather, two-seat attack aircraft. The initial $38m contract saved the firm, but it also pressed McDonnell to experiment with new technology. The aircraft was re-named AH-1 (their first "attack" design) without specific design parameters from the USN, whose attack mission objective actually required a larger aircraft, which became the North American A-5 Vigilante. AH-1 was reallocated to the Navy's fighter design branch in December 1954, where it remained a vague project until July 1955.

Meanwhile, Barkey's team had drafted numerous F3H-G/H variations. The introduction of *Forrestal*-class supercarriers allowed space for larger aircraft, and this inspired David S. Lewis, the project director, to explore multimission design options. Retaining the AH-1 attack capability, his team devised cost-saving interchangeable nose sections to convert the aircraft from a single-seat, gun-armed attacker to a photo-reconnaissance or ECM (electronic countermeasures) platform. Two-seat noses offered training, advanced ECM or airstrike coordination versions. Although nose-changing aboard a carrier was soon deemed impractical, the idea of concentrating mission-adapted electronics for radar interception, reconnaissance, or strike missions in the forward fuselage simplified the production of gun-fighter, reconnaissance, and ECM versions of the Phantom in later years.

To avoid "Demonic" powerplant problems, the designers initially drafted two versions: the F3H-G with the proven J65 engine (a license-built British Armstrong Siddeley Sapphire turbojet), and the better-performing F3H-H with the General Electric J79 developed for the USAF's Mach 2 B-58A Hustler bomber. The US Navy placed their long lead-time J79 order in 1954 and the engine accrued considerable hours in its first service platform, the Lockheed F-104 Starfighter, by the end of 1956. In all, 17,000 examples were produced in 17 versions, including license-built units in Japan, Europe, Canada, and Israel. For the Phantom, it proved to be an extraordinarily reliable, hardy, driving force. The US Navy anticipated that the combined thrust of two J79s would confer excellent climb-to-interception performance and maneuverability in the vertical plane. The unveiling in September 1954 of the Soviet MiG-19, thought to be capable of Mach 1.5, required equivalent speed from the McDonnell design.

Superior air-to-air performance became the main priority for the McDonnell designers from April 1955, when the Navy announced that it needed a fleet defense fighter rather than an AH-1-type attacker. From that point the term F4H-1 was used to define this aircraft, which would patrol near a carrier group, extending loiter time by using one engine and then responding at supersonic speed to threats from high-flying attackers delivering nuclear bombs or stand-off missiles. Attack capability was to be deleted, but fortunately the design was already too far advanced for this to be economical and the airframe retained five structural hard-points that would be the basis for the Phantom's ordnance-carrying muscle. The Navy's fighter branch also specified all-weather performance, requiring complex electronics. Lewis's team felt that this implied a second crew member, a decision reinforced by pressure from the USN guided missile branch in June 1956 to make the Sperry Sparrow III missile the primary armament, with backup from Sidewinder short-range missiles and a gun. An April 1957 revision deleted the gun, a widespread move in aircraft design at that time as it was felt that aerial combat would be conducted at long range with missiles rather than through "dogfighting." Interceptors faced bombers flying well above the fighters' service ceiling, requiring long-range missiles fired from a "snap-up" zoom climb by the interceptor.

F4H-1 BuNo 149405 (USAF serial 62-12168), one of a pair of Production Block 9 aircraft borrowed as F-110As for TAC's 120-day evaluation in 1962. Another 27 F4H-1s were loaned to initiate the USAF training program at McDill AFB. Carriage of AIM-7D Sparrow missiles on the inboard pylons and four fuselage stations shows the Naval Phantom II's primary interception role. (McDonnell Aircraft Company)

These US Navy requirements were built into the design, which still included multimission possibilities. In June 1955 a USN requirement was issued for a two-seat, all-weather fighter for missile-armed interception, and a contract for seven F4H-1 prototypes followed in July. Rather than taking the long route of flight-testing a series of airframe changes to the F3H-H baseline model, Barkey and Lewis had invested heavily in wind-tunnel testing and computers since 1954. After testing 75 wing designs, the F3H wing-sweep angle was retained but the outer wing was thinned. A Demon/Voodoo-like rear fuselage was clad in heat-resistant titanium. The fuselage was given the contoured "coke bottle" area rule profile recommended by the National Advisory Committee on Aeronautics (NACA), reducing drag-induced buffeting at transonic speeds. A stability augmentation system was designed to defeat "roll coupling", when oscillations in both roll and yaw if a pilot turned at supersonic speed could throw the aircraft out of control. A larger, thinner vertical stabilizer, built partly from innovative honeycomb structures, also added directional stability, overcoming a problem that had caused the loss of many early supersonic fighters. In addition the outer wing panels were given 12 degrees of dihedral, partly to overcome a small anhedral angle in the overall wing structure but mainly to enhance stability in a rolling maneuver. The horizontal stabilizer (stabilator) was then canted downwards, further increasing roll stability.

The F4H-1's other distinctive visual feature, its pendulous radome, was lacking from the first example that began ground tests in April 1958. The first two prototypes were built to take the Westinghouse APQ-50 search and track radar that McDonnell had used in the Demon and F2H-3 Banshee. Inadequate detection range using the 24-inch diameter antenna originally specified meant that a larger, 32-inch antenna was used for a revised radar, redesignated APQ-72. The increased size demanded an unprecedentedly large fibreglass radome fabricated by the Virginia-based Brunswick Company. Robert Little made the first F4H-1 flight on May 16, 1958. Mach 1.3 was achieved on the third flight, and testing moved to Edwards AFB. Modified air intakes improved the innovative variable-geometry's supersonic airflow, but the aircraft proved its basic soundness despite its technical complexity. On July 3, 1959, the McDonnell Aircraft Company's 20th anniversary, James Smith McDonnell, company president and chairman, named the F4H-1 "Phantom II."

While the Navy prepared to accept its potent new fighter, in 1958 McDonnell was already approaching the US Air Force about a potential

By the time that this F-4C-18-MC (63-7526) reached the 15th TFW at McDill AFB, Florida in June 1964, McDonnell had already built 547 Phantoms, including 121 F-4Cs. This TAC wing detached its 45th TFS to Ubon RTAFB, Thailand between April 4 and August 10, 1965, a deployment that included the USAF's first Phantom II combat strike missions and first two MiG kills. (R. Besecker via Norman Taylor) ground-attack version with a new bombing radar installation. However, it was the F4H-1's multimission potential, demonstrated in tests, that attracted USAF interest. Initially its superior performance compared with the primary USAF interceptor, the Convair F-106A, came into focus. Lt Gen Tom Miller, supervizing the F4H-1 program for the US Marines, recalled:

> Air Defense Command (ADC) first became interested in the F4H-1. Col Graham was permitted to fly the F4H-1 very early in the program and he pushed it for ADC versus the F-106. His effort culminated in a fly-off between the two aircraft [Project Highspeed], which showed the F4H-1 to be a far superior fighter. It was during a Pentagon debrief of the results of the competition between the F-106 and F4H-1 that Admiral Pirie [in charge of the air-to-ground aspect of the program] offered to provide USAF tactical air operations with an F4H-1 bombing demonstration. I came away from the meeting with the impression that that the USAF personnel were very impressed with the fighter capabilities of the F4H-1 and that caused Admiral Pirie to bring up its bombing capabilities.

The USN was already planning to show off the Phantom II's conventional weapons delivery using multiple bomb racks that were unavailable to the Air Force at the time. Major General Hal Vincent (a captain at the time) ran the O/V 5 air-to-ground tests supervised by Admiral Pirie within the Navy's VX-5 test squadron. He was using F4H-1 BuNo 143390, the fifth Phantom II, for tests with the Mk 7 nuclear special weapon, but "I hung a multiple bomb rack (MBR) on the centerline of the aircraft and I cut another in half, rewired it and made a triple ejector rack for the other two stations, allowing carriage of 24 500lb bombs." Photographs of the original high-drag MBR configuration were circulated by McDonnell and attracted international interest in the Phantom's attack possibilities. Tom Miller was ordered to make a "Nav Tac" demonstration drop of 22 500lb bombs on the Camp Lejeune range at MCAS Cherry Point on April 25, 1961, but further "performances" were requested, witnessed by several congressmen and one of the USAF's most influential policy-shapers, General Curtis Le May. Tom Miller: "They were so impressed that they stole [the Phantom II] away from Air Defense Command. The F-106 remained in ADC and the Phantom II was bought for Tactical Air Command."

Promotion of the Phantom's conventional weapons capability fitted well with the policies of John F. Kennedy, the US president from January 1961. His Secretary of Defense, Robert S. McNamara, believed in the cost-effectiveness of missiles and sought "commonality" in funding versatile equipment that could be used by most of the United States's armed services. In 1960 General Maxwell D. Taylor had written *The Uncertain Trumpet*, in which he argued that the government's 1950s focus on massive nuclear retaliation, with Strategic Air Command as its principal exponent, endangered national security by failing to provide for the more likely conventional war scenarios that emerged beneath the nuclear "umbrella." Kennedy agreed and devised a policy of "flexible response" to meet a range of potential threats, requiring a $3.5m increase in the defense budget. One of the beneficiaries was Hal Vincent's O/V 5 project, which, he recalls, was "showered with money" to develop the Phantom II's conventional ordnance delivery. Meanwhile, as the aircraft began to enter US Navy and Marine Corps service, the crews' training syllabuses focussed on interception but also contained substantial air-to-ground training. The Navy's first Phantom II squadron completed carrier qualifications in October 1961 and the Marines received F4H-1s from June 1962.

General Electric's SUU-16/A and SUU-32/A gun-pods satisfied Phantom pilots' desire for a weapon that would keep heads down ahead of an attack run or provide credible close-in air-to-air shooting power. Remote-control range testing of this SUU-16/A involved removal of the rear and lower sections of the pod's casing, with plenty of restraining cables for the test Phantom. (USAF)

McNamara implemented "flexible response" by seeking a 50 percent increase in the USAF's tactical airpower. The existing wide range of fighter-bombers and light bombers was to be replaced with just two new types, the A-7 Corsair II and General Dynamics F-111, both of which would also be used by Navy squadrons. Because neither of these would be available until at least 1966, he sought a stop-gap fighter-bomber. To McNamara the Phantom II offered both superior performance (proven by the seven world height and speed records attained by F4H-1s by the end of 1961) and also fulfilled his aim of multimission, cost-saving "commonality." However, despite its obvious qualities, overcoming Air Force preconceptions about buying an aircraft used by a rival service required considerable persuasion by both McNamara and McDonnell's sales team. In August 1961, two F4H-1s were borrowed for tests at Edwards AFB and flown to Tactical Air Command (TAC) bases by Col Graham and charismatic F-100 wing commander Col George Laven so that USAF pilots could sample the goods. This was followed by an official fly-off competition against TAC's premier strike fighter, the F-105D Thunderchief, in November 1961. Both types had projected reconnaissance versions in development, which the USAF also required, and both achieved similar results in the set tests, but McNamara's purposes were best served by selecting the Phantom II.

President Kennedy's January 1962 budget requested funding for both fighter and reconnaissance versions of the Phantom II. To assuage USAF pride they were initially called F-110A and RF-110A (nicknamed "Spectre"), following the Air Force's existing "Century Series" fighter designations. To hasten service introduction, 27 more Phantom IIs were reserialed 62-12170/-12196 for USAF training and evaluation with the 4453rd CCTW at McDill AFB, Florida. The first aircraft was flown in by Col Stanton Smith on February 11, 1963, by which time McNamara's September 18, 1962 universal revision of aircraft designations was in effect and the F4H-1 became the F-4B. In April 1962 the first order for an F-110A (62-12199) was placed with McDonnell, followed on May 29 by another for two YRF-110A reconnaissance prototypes (62-12200 and 62-12201). Like the F4H-1, they received new designations, F-4C Phantom II for the F-110A Spectre and YRF-4C for the recce prototypes.

The first of 583 definitive F-4Cs made its maiden flight on May 27, 1963, and production continued until May 4, 1966. Changes to the F-4B basis were minimal, although TAC was already planning improved ground-attack capability for the type. Some of the first F-4Cs joined the borrowed F-4Bs at McDill AFB, where the 12th TFW became the first active USAF Phantom II wing, achieving operational capability in October 1964.

The USAF's need for a reconnaissance version of the Phantom in some ways predated its engagement with the F-4C program, and its Specific Operational Requirement (SOR) for the RF-4C was issued in May 1962, three months before a similar SOR for the production-standard F-4C. Its Republic RF-84F Thunderflash and Douglas RB-66 had been in use since early 1954. The RF-84F provided relatively short-range, "cameras only" reconnaissance, while the RB-66 carried more sophisticated equipment but lacked the performance and agility to operate over high-threat environments. McDonnell's own RF-101 Voodoo, in service from 1957, was a short-term solution, offering supersonic performance and longer range, but was equipped only with cameras. In the RF-4C McDonnell was able to combine superior range and supersonic performance with day and night photo-reconnaissance and a sophisticated suite of sideways-looking radar, infrared, and laser-imaging devices.

Two F-4Bs (62-12200/01) were converted into YRF-4Cs (Model 98DF) with an extended camera nose and blanked-off AIM-7 missile wells, and the first was flown on August 8, 1963, only three months after the first F-4C. A fully equipped production version followed in May 1964, and early examples equipped the 4415th CCTS of Shaw AFB's 363rd TRW in South Carolina that September. The Air Force bought 503 RF-4Cs with deliveries continuing until January 1974, while USMC RF-4B (F4H-1P) production was limited to 46 from 1965, an indication of the way that the USAF took over the Phantom II project from 1964 onwards.

At McDonnell's St Louis factory, F-4C production increased to 340 per year as 18 TAC wings were progressively reequipped, plus a number of test squadrons and one ADC fighter interceptor squadron, the 57th FIS at Keflavik, Iceland later in the F-4C's career. The designers' attention switched to a version that was more attuned to the USAF's strike roles, the F-4D. Service experience had shown the new fighter to be an exceptional combat aircraft with few vices. Structurally, some cracks had occurred in outer wing panels, and the potting compound used on electrical connectors had proven unsatisfactory and was replaced. Fuel leaks from the wing tanks sometimes necessitated frequent resealing and radars, still relying on pre-solid state technology, required a considerable maintenance effort. Although the F-4 had a far better safety record than its Century Series predecessors, from the aircrews' viewpoint there were two particular shortcomings. Primarily, there was the "Phantom thing," a tendency to enter a stall/spin condition if the pilot put too much "g" on the aircraft at high angles of attack, particularly in aerial combat. Spanish F-4C pilots called it the "hachazo" (axe-blow) and it cost them three F-4C crews' lives. Below 10,000ft there was insufficient time for the aircraft to be recovered from this condition. The solution came

The front instrument panel of F-4C-18-MC 63-7428 at the Minnesota ANG Museum. At the top, centrally, is the radar scope with the attitude directional indicator (ADI or artificial horizon) and horizontal situation indicator vertically below it. The radar altimeter and airspeed indicator are the two larger, circular dials to the left of the ADI and the standard altimeter is to its right. The RWR threat warning indicator is above the left coaming section. (Gary Chambers)

through training, but the second deficiency, the lack of an internal gun, was the result of long-term design policies and was not properly remedied until the F-4E variant was flown in August 1965.

While all-missile armament was appropriate for the Navy's interception role, TAC could see that USAF ground-attack missions would generate greater need for a gun. Suppression of ground fire, attacks on troop concentrations, and close-in air-to-air use could be foreseen in "limited war" scenarios such as Southeast Asia as early as 1963, when interest in an integral gun was first expressed. By 1965, Vietnam experience showed that there was a real need for guns and by October the General Electric M61A-1 rotary cannon, already successful in fighters like the F-104 and F-105, was approved for trial installation in a new Phantom, the F-4E. While this, the most numerous USAF F-4, was developed, an improved F-4C was ordered, although contracts for it had been issued within weeks of the first F-4C deliveries.

The F-4D incorporated changes that brought the Phantom closer to USAF needs without major external changes. Following its Category I acceptance tests in 1966, the usual Category II and III tests were curtailed as the aircraft was so urgently required in Vietnam. In addition to its improved ground-attack capability using an ASQ-91 weapons-release computer, it was wired on the production line for the SUU-16/A or SUU-23/A gun-pod, mounted on the centerline. General Electric SUU-16/As had been used in combat, initially by the 8th TFW, as a way of mounting an M61 Vulcan cannon on the F-4 for air-to-ground engagements. It also proved successful in aerial combat, and ten MiGs were destroyed by pod-armed Phantoms over North Vietnam from May 1967. Combat use ended in late 1968. Air-to-air missiles proved to be far from reliable in combat ("miss-iles" rather than "hit-iles," as one frustrated crewman put it) and pilots welcomed a backup weapon. However, the gun-pod was heavy, it used up the 600-gallon tank pylon, its mounting was not sufficiently stable to ensure lasting alignment and accuracy, and its extending ram-air turbine power source limited its use to speeds below 350kts. It also tended to jam.

Mounting the gun internally obviated most of these difficulties, and this had been suggested by McDonnell from 1961 onwards, either as a nose-mounted weapon or attached to a rear missile well as a "gun module" containing an M61 and 1200 rounds. Acceptance of the nose-mount location for an F-4E TSF (tactical strike fighter) variant in June 1965 paralleled development of a new radar, the Westinghouse AN/APQ-120(V) (an upgraded AN/APQ-109.) This light-weight, solid-state unit required a smaller scanner, allowing a more pointed nose, extended by 33 inches, and more space to fit the Vulcan cannon and its ammunition drum. At first, engineers used a version that had worked well in the Republic F-105, but the ammunition feed system did not operate properly in the F-4 and redesign was needed. The gun's proximity to the aircraft's radar and other sensitive electronics caused vibration, requiring extensive damping.

A trial gun installation was tested in the YRF-4C prototype 62-12200, replacing the cameras and projecting through the forward/oblique camera window. An AN/APG-30 radar and A4 lead-computing gun sight were fitted for trials as the YF-4E, which also tested prototypes of the J79-GE-10 for the Navy's new F-4 and J79-GE-17 for the production F-4E. These uprated engines each generated an extra 900lb of thrust and were eventually given a much-needed smoke reduction option. Two more YRF-4Cs were converted, 63-7445 (a former F-4C) and 65-0713 (an F-4D), to refine the gun and radar installations and to establish the correct contours for the nose rather than adapting the flat-sided RF-4C profile. The extra weight in the nose was balanced by an additional 84-gallon fuel tank (number 7) in the rear fuselage. Overall weight reduction was effected by deleting the naval wing-folding mechanism that had been retained in the F-4C/D and the little-used pop-out ram-air turbine that was intended to provide backup generator power. This was later replaced by a small auxiliary power unit in the rear fuselage. Cross-fertilization from the last USN variant, the F-4J, resulted in an improved jet nozzle with longer "turkey feather" afterburner "petals" for the J79-GE-17 engine and a slot on the leading edge of the stabilator, increasing its effectiveness particularly at lower airspeeds.

Production was approved on July 22, 1966 and by June 30, 1967 the definitive F-4E-31-MC (66-0284) was ready to fly, although several items of equipment were not yet installed. One of the principal reasons for the F-4E program was the Hughes CORDS (coherent on receive doppler system), using the APQ-120 radar and Hughes airborne missile control sub-system (AMCS). This advanced system was intended to improve the APQ-120's performance

A slatted-wing F-4E with six Mk 82s on the centerline pylon, two AIM-9J Sidewinders on LAU-105 rails attached to the right inboard pylon, and a GBU-10 on the opposite pylon. The left forward Sparrow missile well houses an AVQ-23 Pave Spike laser designator pod. MiG-killer pilot Gordon Clouser remarked "I preferred the F-4E. Coming from the F-105 Thunderchief, in my biased opinion any fighter without a gun is not a fighter." (McDonnell Douglas)

F-4G-43-MC 69-7212 of the 52nd TFW carries an inert AGM-88 HARM in August 1991, although the five "scores" on its intake plate indicate successful live firings during the Gulf War earlier that year. The missile has an adapter beam and the pylon installation is angled slightly outwards to clear the main landing gear. An AN/ALE-40 chaff/flare dispenser is attached to the rear of the pylon. (Author)

against low-flying targets in conditions of "ground clutter," providing a clearer image for a missile shot against an aircraft as low as 100ft above ground. CORDS ran ahead of the available computer hardware and had to be abandoned in 1968, but a revised APQ-120 was installed in production F-4Es and retrofitted to the first batch of 26 aircraft. Also absent from the first Block 31–33 aircraft was the radar homing and warning (RHAW) system to protect them from enemy SAM (surface-to-air missiles) and other radars. The Bendix AN/APR-107 set originally prescribed for the F-4E proved unreliable and ATI AN/APR-36 and APR-37 units were substituted in production aircraft, with the improved ATI digital AN/ALR-46 system replacing these from the mid-1970s. ALR-46 could be quickly reprogrammed before a mission to tackle threats that might be faced that day.

While all the black boxes were being sorted out, the first F-4E (66-0286) for the 4525th FWW at Nellis AFB was delivered on October 3, 1967 to begin the training program. Other examples reached the first operational TAC wing, the 33rd TFW, at Eglin AFB the following month. By November 1968 F-4Es were replacing the F-105Ds of the 388th TFW at Korat RTAFB, Thailand and flying combat missions over Laos. The F-4E became the USAF's principal Phantom model and the most widely exported variant. In all, 1,389 were built, of which many were later loaned, transferred, or sold to Greece, Egypt, Iran, Turkey, Israel, Australia, and South Korea. Another 140 were supplied to Japan or built under license by Mitsubishi from 1971 and operated by the

F-4F-53-MC72-1130 72-1130, 37+20 OF JG73 STEINHOFF, 1997

The camouflage pattern is Norm 81B using RAL 7012 Basaltgrau, 7009 Grungrau, 7030 Steingrau, and 7037 Staugrau, with 7030 Steingrau and 7035 Lichtgrau undersurfaces. The black radome indicates that the aircraft has received the first two stages of the Peace Rhine/ICE program, optimizing it for air-to-ground operations for which it would also carry AGM-65 Maverick among other ordnance. JG73 was re-named from JBG35 in 1993 and reestablished at Rostock-Laage AB, operating with former East German AF MiG-29s before converting to the Eurofighter in 2004.

Japanese Air Self-Defense Force as the F-4EJ, with 14 RF-4EJ reconnaissance models added in 1974. West Germany ordered 150 RF-4Es and 175 F-4Fs, a modified F-4E with part-manufacture of the airframes and license-building of the J79-GE-17A engines undertaken by German firms. All these countries invested heavily in the F-4E, and it has been the subject of numerous update programs to extract the longest possible service life from each airframe.

In USAF service the F-4E received a number of improvements in the light of combat experience in Vietnam. As a missile-armed interceptor the F-4 was never intended to engage in close combat with enemy fighters, yet over Vietnam there were frequent fights with more agile MiG-17s, MiG-19s, and MiG-21s. While Phantom crews had maintained an acceptable degree of superiority over these adversaries, it was clear that a more maneuverable F-4 would increase the kill rate in combat and also reduce losses through stall-spin "departures" in high-g maneuvering, which caused the loss of almost 200 F-4s in all. From 1958 onwards it had been suggested that slats on the leading edges of the wings of land-based F-4s could replace the blown-flap system that had been installed to improve the naval Phantoms' low-speed handling for aircraft-carrier recovery. Studies at McDonnell Douglas (the two firms merged in 1967) had been undertaken in the early design phases for the F-4's successor, the F-15 Eagle, although in the end slats were not required for the new fighter.

Once again, McDonnell's test-bed Phantom 62-12200 was enlisted, and it was fitted with maneuvering slats in 1969. Supporting trials in Israel with a similarly modified F-4E showed that the stall-spin condition could be abated in hard turns, and combat maneuverability was improved though top speed fell by 80kt. After various slat configurations had been tested in the Agile Eagle 1 and 2 initiatives, a definitive slat arrangement was installed in F-4E 66-0287 using hydraulically powered slats on both outer and inner wing panels. F-4Es from aircraft 71-0237 in production block 48 onwards had slats installed "on the line" and retrofit kits were supplied to modify 304 F-4Es with the original "hard" wing.

Although McDonnell Douglas built reconnaissance versions of the F-4E as the RF-4E for an offset sales agreement with Germany, no funding was available to replace the USAF fleet of RF-4Cs with the more fuel-efficient J79-GE-17-powered RF-4E. However, one final major evolution of the F-4E design was allowed when 116 USAF F-4Es were converted to F-4G "Wild Weasels." Soviet SA-2 Guideline air-to-ground missiles proved to be deadly adversaries for US air forces in Vietnam, shooting down 195 aircraft and requiring a considerable effort in devising adequate countermeasures. SAM-suppression equipment was operationally tested in F-100F Super Sabres and then installed in F-105F/G Thunderchief "Wild Weasels," which achieved considerable success with their electronic countermeasures and specially developed antiradiation missiles. As F-105 production had ceased in December 1964 in favour of the F-4D, it was clear that losses of F-105 Wild Weasels would have to be met by a Phantom conversion. The first attempt was a batch of 36 Wild Weasel IV F-4Cww or "EF-4C" conversions in 1968, but the aircraft's dense internal structure precluded the effective installation of the necessary electronics, including provision for the AGM-78, the most effective of the available anti-SAM weapons.

F-105Gs (Wild Weasel IV) and EF-4Cs provided SEAD (suppression of enemy air defenses) during the final stages of the Vietnam War, but the quest for a Wild Weasel V received a major boost in 1973. Over 30 Israeli Air Force Phantoms were destroyed by Soviet SAMs and radar-directed ZSU-23 AAA (antiaircraft artillery) during the brutal Yom Kippur conflict that autumn when American ECM equipment in the Israeli aircraft provided insufficient protection. McDonnell and IBM had tested a new homing and warning computer, the AN/APR-38, in two F-4Ds in 1973 but internal space limitations prevented adequate installation. Attention turned to the F-4E, but even there the only viable installation area was to be found by removing the M61 gun, with other components in a fin-top pod. This proposal was successfully tested in F-4E 69-7254, and 134 F-4Es were subsequently converted to F-4Gs. The aircraft gained AGM-78 Standard ARM capability and it could still handle all the F-4E's external ordnance. It entered squadron service in April 1978. Together with General Dynamics EF-111A Raven and USN EA-6B Prowlers, the USAF's F-4Gs led the Operation *Desert Storm* air campaign in 1991, speedily disposing of Iraq's air defenses. This F-4G force was living on borrowed time though. Its retirement was delayed by participation in the first Iraq war, but six years later the final combat sortie was flown on January 2, 1996. Retirement from active service for these, the last USAF Phantoms, was signaled by the final sortie by an Idaho ANG F-4G on April 20 of the same year, 34 years after the first USAF funding was allocated for the F-4.

Whereas 1950s fighter aircraft were expected to last for a few years before being replaced, the F-4 showed that in an age of far more costly warplanes a sound design could be updated and adapted to new roles, still holding its own alongside more recent types. Service life extension programs (SLEP), such as those for Japan's F-4EJ Kai, Israel's Kurnass 2000, Germany's F-4F ICE, and Turkey's Phantom 2020, have combined advanced digital electronics developed for a later generation of fighters like the F/A-18 Hornet with refurbished F-4 airframes. This has enabled the Phantom to handle a wider range of guided weapons, such as the AIM-120 AMRAAM missile, using more powerful and reliable radars and fire-control systems. Many of these projects have been undertaken by foreign Phantom users, as McDonnell Douglas, from the 1970s onwards, wanted to promote its new products such as the F-15 Eagle and F/A-18 Hornet. In 1967 the company did draft a radical, short-lived proposal for a swing-wing F-4J (FV)S as an alternative to the

Grumman F-14 Tomcat. However, Boeing Military Airplane Company (BMAC), which merged with McDonnell Douglas in 1997, proposed another "Super Phantom." Reengined with Pratt and Whitney PW1120 turbofans, this F-4E derivative had a 1,100-gallon conformal fuel and weapons tank beneath most of the fuselage, and avionics drawn from the F-16, F/A-18, and Northrop F-20 programs. The PW1120 was installed in a demonstrator and it generated 30 percent more afterburning thrust and weighed 25 percent less, with a potential 18 percent range increase. Although the engine promised spectacular performance improvements, this proposal failed to find customers and funding was terminated in 1986.

TECHNICAL SPECIFICATIONS

Airframe

Fuselage
Aircraft carrier operations required a strong, resilient airframe and the USAF Phantom variants all benefited from its naval origins. During the eight-month building process the fuselage was constructed in three sections. The forward fuselage was split vertically, with most of the wiring and ducting inbuilt before the halves were joined. It included the forward air intake ducts, their ramp actuators, and rigid, machined intake leading edges. The perforated forward ramp let boundary layer air bleed off and exhaust overboard, while its solid rear section was positioned by the air data computer to provide optimum airflow at high speeds. Tandem, pressurized cockpits with two Martin Baker Mk H5 ejection seats (later replaced by the Mk H7 rocket-powered, zero-zero model), the nose undercarriage well, and the Number One fuel cell occupied most of the space, together with denser structures including the radar, cabin air-conditioning, oxygen system, and other avionics. Re-contoured noses, extended by 4.75ft, housed the reconnaissance equipment for the RF-4 versions or the gun for the F-4E/F. The radar scanner, 32 inches in diameter in the F-4C/D but smaller for RF-4/F-4E variants, was housed in a neoprene-covered fibreglass radome.

In the 22ft-long centre section were the two engine compartments with a central dividing keel, six fuel cells (five in the F-4C/D), and access doors for the engines and fuel system. Whereas the forward fuselage was mainly aluminum, a variety of alloy, titanium, and stainless steel components coped with the high temperatures in the central fuselage. The rear fuselage (mostly made by Republic Aviation Corporation) supported the three-spar vertical fin and rudder and the one-piece horizontal stabilator. The latter, with 35 degrees sweepback and 23.25 degrees anhedral, had titanium inner sections to resist the heat from the engine efflux passing directly beneath it. Its drooped configuration provided good longitudinal and directional stability and counteracted the upswept outer wing panels' tendency to make the aircraft roll during a yawing maneuver. Its location saved structural weight in the vertical fin compared with the high-mounted position McDonnell had used for their F-101 Voodoo, and it prevented the stabilator from being "blanked off" by the wing at high angles of attack. It also acted as an air-brake if fully depressed after touch-down on landing.

Stabilator and rudder operation used a traditional system of push/pull-rods, bell-cranks and cables, with a stall warning mechanism that vibrated the pilot's left rudder pedal. An aileron/rudder interconnect (ARI) moved the rudder proportionately to the ailerons, allowing smooth, coordinated turns at lower airspeeds. The rudder became effective at about 70kt on take-off. A compartment at the end of the fuselage housed the 16-foot ring-slot brake parachute, deployable below 200kt. The lower keel area between the jet-pipes comprised a double-wall structure with innovative titanium skins, asbestos insulation, and ram-air cooling protected by an additional layer of titanium shingles. All F-4s had the naval arresting hook attached to the central fuselage keel area, actuated by hydraulic pressure.

Wing and flight controls

The basic F-4 wing was a multi-spar structure with 45 degrees of sweepback. A torque-box structure, extending outwards to the wing-fold line where the outer panels were attached, was sealed to form a fuel tank. Canted upwards at 12 degrees, each outer panel folded upwards, another inherited naval characteristic. The skins for this wing-box were expensively milled to taper from the wing-root outwards as a weight-saving measure. Hydraulic three-position flaps were attached to the trailing edge of the inner wing section. Ailerons fitted outboard of the flaps were synchronized with two spoilers above each inner wing section. The ailerons deflected fully down by 30 degrees individually but upwards by only 1 degree, while the spoilers could rise up to 45 degrees, so that in order to bank to the right, the left aileron was depressed and the right spoiler was raised. With flaps lowered the ailerons both automatically depressed by 10 degrees, but continued to behave as ailerons. For take-off the pilot selected "HALF" on his flap lever, dropping the leading edge flaps by the full 60 degrees and the trailing edge flaps by 30 degrees. Flaps and slats tended to "chatter," or vibrate on extension, maneuvering, or retraction, audible as brief electronic interference on the pilot's headphones.

On "hard-wing" (unslatted) Phantoms, "HALF" also engaged BLC (boundary layer control) for the leading edge flaps. The "DOWN" position

While "wonder arch" shelters are constructed to protect aircraft from Viet Cong rocket attacks, RF-4C-25-MC 65-0840 sits in an open 12th TRS revetment. The squadron flew combat missions from Tan Son Nhut AB from 1966 to 1971. Ahead of the all-moving, unslotted stabilator with its heat-resistant titanium inner section, the closed doors of the photoflash cartridge ejectors can be seen. The outboard ailerons (or, more accurately, "flaperons") drooped without hydraulic pressure. (USAF)

on the flap control, used for landing, also set the trailing edge flaps at 60 degrees and switched in their BLC too. The BLC system, deleted for the F-4E/G, drew hot air from the 17th compressor stages of both engines, piping it out over the flaps and giving the effect of improved air-flow over the wing and lower stalling speed. A hinged, hydraulic speed-brake opened below each wing, operated by two switches on the throttle control. In wartime, antiradar chaff could be dropped from the speed-brake wells. There were two pylon hard-points on each wing.

Three separate hydraulic systems operated at 300lb psi: PC1 and PC2 to power the ailerons, stabilator and spoilers via a pump attached to each engine, and a utility system to power flaps, undercarriage, rudder, wing-fold (where applicable), arresting hook, and nose-wheel steering. Despite the mutual backup arrangement of the three systems, hydraulic failure, particularly after combat damage, was a common source of lost F-4s. However, a further emergency pneumatic system provided backup power to the flaps, undercarriage, and wheel brakes if the hydraulics failed. The inward-retracting main undercarriage wheels had tires inflated to 200 psi.

Engines

With a production run of over 17,000 units, the General Electric J79 was one of the most successful turbojet engines of its time and its designers won the 1958 Collier Trophy. Aircraft using the engine set 46 new world performance records and it remained in production for over 30 years. License production of 3,249 for overseas users of the F-4 and F-104 Starfighter was undertaken by Bet Shemesh Engines in Israel (also for the IAI Kfir fighter), MTU Aero Engines in Germany, Ishikawajima-Harima Heavy Industries in Japan, Orenda Engines in Canada, and a consortium of Alfa Romeo, Fiat, and Fabrique Nationale in Europe. Weighing 3,850lb, the 19ft 4inch-long powerplant offered light weight and up to 17,900lb of afterburning thrust. Its single-spool turbojet design, including a 17-stage compressor with costly stainless steel blades, was innovative in using stator vanes whose angle could be varied

General Electric's J79 engine was produced for over 30 years in various, similar versions for the F-4, F-104, B-58A Hustler, A-5 Vigilante, F11F-1F, IAI Kfir, and in its J79-119 version (with a sharper "bullet" fairing) for the GD F-16/79. Modular construction simplified maintenance. GE boasted that early J79s sustained less than one in-flight shutdown problem per 100,000 flight hours. (General Electric Company)

according to the aircraft's angle of attack. This enabled the engine to develop as much thrust as a twin-spool engine but with lower weight and complexity and reduced compressor stalling. The J79 opened the way for a whole generation of high-thrust, low-weight engines.

A major component in the successful combination of J79 engine and F-4 airframe was the very effective air intake system. McDonnell designed one of the first variable geometry systems, using ramps that varied the intake cross-section to control the speed and volume of airflow and a perforated bell-mouth ring ahead of the compressor, regulating the amount of air that bypassed the engine and reducing a build-up of air and consequent stall. Smooth airflow and controllable pressure were therefore maintained for air entering the engine. As hot gases passed through the engine and afterburner section, where they were mixed with raw JP4 fuel to give a massive thrust increase, they also passed through McDonnell's convergent/divergent jet nozzles. At that point the jet efflux was mixed at the "convergent" nozzle (the inner "ring" of the rear engine as seen from behind the aircraft) with bypass air that had flowed around the engine giving additional cooling. Gases then passed through the "divergent" nozzle (the outer part of the tail-pipe), which controlled the speed of the air-mass as it left the aircraft. The volume of cooling air drawn into the jet efflux was sufficient to prevent the afterburner heat from damaging the engine casing. Afterburners could be modulated through four stages of extra thrust, a big advance on the "on/off" afterburners of earlier fighters.

The engine oil tank held 6 gallons, burned at about one pint per hour. In combat, the engine's main disadvantage was its dense smoke-trail, visible from up to 20 miles. It could be reduced by using minimum afterburner on one engine and "idle" power on the other in cruise flight. A minor upgrade that increased burn temperature by about 10 degrees could eliminate the smoke-trail, but this reduced engine life and was seldom installed.

Fuel system

The F-4C's six fuselage tanks held 1,342 gallons of JP4 with another 630 gallons in two internal wing tanks. Additional avionics in the RF-4C and F-4D occupied some No 1 fuselage tank space, reducing overall fuel capacity to 1,259 gallons. The F-4E added a seventh fuselage tank but other reductions in tank size kept overall fuselage capacity to 1,225 gallons. A further 600 gallons were available in an external Royal Jet tank below the fuselage (a "ferry" tank that wasn't stressed for combat) and 740 gallons in two McDonnell or Sargent Fletcher external wing tanks, each cleared for Mach 1.6. Exact sequencing of the fuel transfer from all these tanks was necessary to preserve the center of gravity. Emergency fuel dump vents were located on each wing trailing edge. Fuel consumption averaged 190lb per minute, increasing to around 750lb per minute in afterburner.

Armament

Air-to-air missiles and guns
Raytheon/General Dynamics AIM-7 Sparrow III. The Phantom was originally designed around this missile, used by all F-4s excluding the RF-4C/E, with two or four carried in purpose-built fuselage wells. Originating from earlier Sparrow air-to-air missiles dating back to 1946, the AIM-7E was the first mass-produced version in 1963 and the main armament for the original F4H-

1. It was designed to hit large, non-maneuvering targets at high altitude. Widely used with disappointing results in very different circumstances in Vietnam, it was succeeded by a "dogfight" version in 1969, the AIM-7E-2, which had shorter minimum range and improved maneuverability. The AIM-7F, with a bigger warhead, longer range, and a Doppler seeker head, entered service in 1975 aboard F-4E/G Phantoms and was succeeded in 1982 by the AIM-7M with further warhead improvements and a digital monopulse seeker that could avoid locking on to flares ejected by a target aircraft to distract the missile. The AIM-7E weighed 452lb, achieved a peak speed of Mach 3.7, and had a range of up to 28 miles, though rocket burn time could be reduced to around 5 miles in denser, low-altitude air. Its 66lb warhead exploded into 2,500 destructive fragments. Guidance was by a Raytheon continuous wave, semiactive radar linked to the F-4's search radar, which had to "illuminate" the target from missile launch until impact or the radar lock would be broken and the missile would go astray. It was replaced on F-4F ICE and Greek AF Peace Icarus 2000 F-4Es by the Hughes AIM-120 AMRAAM with lighter weight and greatly improved performance.

Ford Aerospace/Raytheon AIM-9 Sidewinder. Used by all F-4s including some RF-4Cs and developed from 1951 onwards, the short-range, heatseeking AIM-9 was the USAF's most successful air-to-air weapon in combat. The first operational version, the AIM-9B, had a 2.6-mile range, a 10lb blast-fragmentation warhead, and 155lb weight, but it could only be fired from directly behind a non-maneuvering, heat-emitting target, unlike later models. Later USAF versions (also used by foreign air forces) were the AIM-9E with a more sensitive Peltier thermo-electric cooler, the AIM-9J with double-delta fins, and the AIM-9L all-aspect version. The AIM-9M and AIM-9P were improved AIM-9Ls, and many of them upgraded earlier missiles as well as new-build. Late AIM-9 variants offered a five-fold range increase over the AIM-9B.

General Electric M61 Vulcan 20mm gun. This was used by F-4E/Fs (internally) with 639 rounds of M50 ammunition and in an SUU-16/A or

The breech door for the F-4E/F's Vulcan gun, opened with two quick-release fasteners and left open preflight to check that a gun safety pin (visible here with its red ribbon) was in place. Other panels revealed the whole gun for maintenance purposes. Above the gun breech is the air scoop for cooling the avionics and cockpit environmental control system. (Author)

Two AIM-7E Sparrows occupy the rear missile wells on this F-4D-33-MC (66-8796) in 1968, while the left forward well houses a Fairchild KB-18 70mm panoramic strike camera for bomb damage assessment. The inboard pylons each hold three SUU-41/A "Gravel" dispensers (used by the 8th TFW), with ten cluster weapon adapters per pod. "Gravel" mines, including the CBU-39/A, CBU-40/A (antipersonnel), or ten CBU-5/B clusters with a total of 7,500 XM40EJ antiintrusion mines per dispenser, were loaded. (Al Piccirillo via Norman Taylor)

SUU-23/A external pod with 1,200 rounds by the F-4C/D. Its six, 5ft-long barrels rotated anticlockwise as a unit, reducing heat and increasing barrel life. Rate of fire was selectable at "low" (4,000) or "high" (6,000 rounds per minute), and the pilot could select a set number of rounds (typically 50) per burst, up to a limit of 3 seconds' firing time to prevent over-heating. Total firing time at 6,000 rounds per minute was about 13 seconds for the internal gun. Electronically primed rounds were drawn from an internal drum (or storage at the rear of the pod) via a linkless feed on a flexible conveyor belt. Spent cases were returned to the drum to preserve the center of gravity.

Hughes AIM-4 Falcon. Dating from 1949, the GAR Falcon family evolved into the AIM-4D (GAR-2B) by 1963. This heatseeking, short-range alternative to the AIM-9 was used by several USAF interceptors and some F-4D/Es. Its complex setup and cooling procedure caused problems for combat use in Vietnam.

Rafael Armament Authority Python 3. An Israeli AIM-9 derivative used from 1977 onwards, this heatseeker with a thermo-cooled IR (infrared) seeker had larger, swept-back tail fins, Mach 3 speed, a 31lb warhead, and all-aspect capability comparable to the AIM-9L.

Air-to-surface guided weapons

Martin Marietta AGM-12 Bullpup. The widely used AGM-12B of 1960 was a redesign of the 1954 ASM-N-7A stand-off, rocket-propelled guided bomb, with a 250lb warhead and a range of 7 miles. It was superseded in 1964 by Bullpup C (AGM-12C) with a 1,000lb warhead. Controlled by a small joystick in the cockpit, the missile had tail-mounted flares for the pilot to guide it visually, but this required him to risk flying directly towards the target until bomb impact.

Hughes/Martin Marietta AGM-62 Walleye. This early glide-bomb was controlled by a nose-mounted TV camera, gyro-stabilized to lock on to a high visual contrast target and allow the carrier aircraft to leave the area, having dropped it from around 35,000ft. It was used by USAF F-4D/Es and Israeli F-4Es. Walleye II was based on a 2,000lb Mk 84 bomb.

A formidable warload of Mk 82 bombs, AIM-7E missiles, and a 571lb AGM-12B Bullpup air-to-ground missile. The "AWOL" nickname on F-4D-32-MC 66-8727's flank indicated the "absence" of its MiG-killing pilot Capt Doyle D. Baker from the US Marine Corps while he was attached to the 13th TFS at Udorn RTAFB in 1967. Guidance flares can be seen at the rear of the missile. (Col Doyle Baker via Peter B. Mersky)

Hughes AGM-65 Maverick. This Bullpup-replacement project, begun in 1965 for service in 1972, included the TV-guided AGM-65A/B and AGM-65D/G with imaging infrared guidance for night-capability, doubled lock-on range, 300lb warhead, and compatibility with the F-4G's APR-38 system. It was also used by the F-4F and F-4Es of Turkey, Israel (as the "Penguin"), and Greece. Effective range is 8–9 miles.

Rafael Armament Authority/Martin Marietta AGM-142A Popeye. Weighing 3,300lb, this stand-off missile required a special inboard pylon adapter and an AN/ASW-55 data pod on the outboard pylon. It was also cleared for Turkish F-4 "Terminator 2020s" and some RoKAF F-4Es.

IMI Gabriel Mk IIA/S. An air-launched, transonic version of an Israeli-produced, sea-skimming, antishipping missile with a 330lb warhead and 25-mile range. Guidance was either fire-and-forget via its own agile radar, through radar control from the launch aircraft, or via datalink from a helicopter. Two of these 12.6ft-long missiles could be carried by Israeli F-4Es.

Texas Instruments AGM-45A Shrike. A US Navy-developed 400lb antiradiation missile, tuned (premission) to particular radar emitters that it could damage or destroy with a 145lb warhead at around 8–15 miles' range. It was used by USAF F-4G, F-4Cww, and Israeli AF F-4E.

B

ORDNANCE/ARMAMENT
1. Rockwell KMU-353A/B (GBU-8/B) HOBOS
2. Ford Aerospace/Raytheon AIM-9L Sidewinder
3. General Electric AN/ALQ-87 ECM pod
4. Rafael Shafrir 2 missile
5. Raytheon/GD AIM-7E-2 Sparrow
6. Hughes AIM-4D Falcon missile
7. Marconi/Tracor QRC-490 chaff dispenser
8. SUU-30/B CBU dispenser
9. Westinghouse AN/ALQ-119(V) ECM pod
10. General Electric SUU-16/A gun-pod
11. Hughes AGM-65B Maverick missile
12. Texas Instruments/Raytheon GBU-12/B
13. Mitsubishi Type 80 ASM-1 missile
14. Hunting Engineering BL755

General Dynamics AGM-78 Standard ARM. Originally, it used Shrike guidance electronics attached to a USN RIM-66 Standard surface-to-air missile, but was air-launched to perform the Shrike function more effectively at up to 50 miles' range with a 214lb warhead. The upgraded AGM-78C/D had new guidance electronics. It was used by USAF F-4Gs and the Israeli Air Force.

Texas Instruments AGM-88A/B/C HARM. A sophisticated replacement for Standard ARM, it was faster, lighter, and had a "broad band" seeker that could be programmed against several SAM sites, either from the F-4G's APR-47 radar warning receiver or before flight when the missile searched out its target, guiding onto the target's emissions. A third mode enabled it to home on to unanticipated targets of opportunity.

The inboard pylon of a JaboG-35 F-4F, with training rounds for the AIM-9 Sidewinder and AGM-65B Maverick. The "scene mag" stencil indicates that the missile's TV guidance system includes a facility to magnify a target image on a cockpit screen, allowing the pilot to see and lock on to smaller targets at greater range, albeit with a rather small field of vision. (Author)

Mitsubishi Type 80 ASM-1C. This 1,345lb medium-range antishipping missile was compatible with the F-4EJ Kai. Powered by a solid-propellant rocket motor, this "fire-and-forget" 684mph weapon combined inertial and radar guidance.

Bombs

F-4s of many air forces have carried a wide range of general-purpose, free-fall bombs including M117 (820lb), Mk 81 (260lb), Mk 82 (510lb), Mk 84 (1,972lb), and retarded versions of the Mk 81 and Mk 82 with extending Mk 15 Snakeye 1 fins. Air-inflatable retarding kits could also be fitted to the Mk 82 AIR, M117 AIR, and Mk 84 AIR. Spanish F-4Cs also carried indigenous ALD-250 and ALD-500 versions of the Mk 82 and Mk 83, among others.

After tests with many different versions, laser-guided adaptations of the Paveway I series GBU-12 (Mk 82-based) and GBU-10A/B (Mk 84) were used in Vietnam by F-4D/Es, and were succeeded by the Paveway II with simpler guidance electronics and pop-out wings that occupied less space than the fixed aerofoils of Paveway I. Paveway III versions of the Mk 84 (GBU-24/B), introduced in 1987, had a digital autopilot and microprocessor controls for

Armed for virtually any eventuality apart from "air-to-air," 81st TFW F-4D-31-MC 66-7735 totes a Rockwell GBU-8/B HOBOS (left). The centerline pylon supports an SUU-23/A gun-pod and the right inboard pylon has a GBU-10 laser-guided bomb. The forward missile wells accommodate an AVQ-23 Pave Spike (left well) and an ALQ-119(V) ECM pod (right, foreground). (Author)

An F-4G with a full complement of SEAD weaponry, including AGM-88B HARMs and AGM-65G Mavericks on LAU-117 launchers, with a pair of AIM-7F Sparrows in the rear wells in case the bad guys appear. A high-g F-15 centerline fuel tank and an AN/ALQ-184(V)1 ECM pod complete the lethal load. (USAF)

use in poor weather and for release at low altitude or in a zoom-climb. The Israeli Aircraft Industries' Griffin and Guillotine were Paveway derivatives, but Israeli F-4s also used GBU-10 and GBU-12A/B (known as Zar'It 82) and the Elbit Opher infrared homing and control package for bombs including the Mk 82.

Laser guidance for Paveway bombs came from a series of designator pods, beginning with the so-called "Zot Box" attached to the rear canopy of 8th TFW F-4Ds in the late 1960s (also to some Iranian AF F-4Ds). Several F-4Ds combat-tested the heavy AVQ-10 Pave Knife designator, which housed laser and low-light TV designators and was intended to work with the aircraft's radar. Other systems, including AVQ-11 Pave Sword, were also tested, and AVQ-23 Pave Spike, using a similar Pave Knife-type TV system in a much smaller pod, became widely used as a daylight-only laser designator for USAF and some South Korean and Turkish AF F-4D/Es. AVQ-26 Pave Tack, the first night-capable laser designator, was mainly associated with the F-111F Aardvark, but some F-4Es were also equipped with it.

Vietnam was the proving ground for a range of electro-optical precision-guided munitions. The first operational model was the Rockwell homing bomb (HOBOS/GBU-8), using the Mk 84 bomb and GBU-9 with a 3,000lb M118E1. An F-4 back-seater locked the launch-and-leave bomb onto a target, and the weapon's KMU-353/A (Mk 84) and KMU-390/B (M118) image-contrast seeker systems guided it on its trajectory. An alternative guidance kit, the KMU-359/B that used infrared imaging, was tested. These weapons were also used by Israeli F-4Es, and they evolved into the GBU-15 Modular Guided Weapon with larger aerofoils to increase range. Like earlier GBUs it used a strap-on guidance package and fin kit attached to a standard bomb, in this case a Mk 84, with datalink control.

Initially, cluster bombs were dispensed from containers (e.g. SUU-7) that remained on the F-4's pylons, but for greater accuracy and reduced drag, free-fall dispensers (e.g. SUU-30) that open out and disperse the "bomblet" submunition contents (e.g. BLU-26/B or BLU-43/B) were devised instead. They were extensively used for tasks ranging from antiaircraft site suppression to

The GBU-15 combined the Maverick missile's electro-optical seeker head with a short-chord or long-chord wing set and Mk 84 bomb. The carrier aircraft used an AXQ-14 datalink pod, attached to its centerline pylon, for bomb guidance. The only F-4 unit to use it was the 3rd TFW, whose TISEO-equipped F-4E-49-MC 71-1087 is seen releasing a long-chord GBU-15 (V)-1. (USAF)

attacks on troop concentrations or delayed-action "seeding" of jungle trails in Laos. The most frequently used of the many cluster bomb munitions have included CBU-58, CBU-87, Mk 20 Rockeye, and CBU-89 Gator combined effects munitions. "Bomblets" were dispensed from a wide range of containers, notably the SUU-7 rearward-ejecting, 19-tube version (Vietnam era) and the SUU-13 downward-dispensing 20-tube model. Each carried a selection of small BLUs (bomb live units), ranging from the BLU-4 antipersonnel/fragmentation to the BLU-24 "jungle bomb." SUU-30 was a widely used cluster bomb using BLU-26 bomblets, CBU-58, and many others. SUU-64/65 tactical munitions dispensers carried CBU-87 and CBU-89 bombs with submunitions such as the BLU-92 antitank mine. The Rafael TAL CBU was used by Israeli F-4s, and the Hunting Engineering BL755 cluster bomb was available for German F-4Fs and Iranian Phantoms for strikes on Iraqi targets.

Other weapons

Nuclear weapons. The B28 (2,030lb), B43 (2,060lb), and particularly the tactical B61 Silver Bullet (710lb) were carried by USAF F-4s during their nuclear alert years. All USAF F-4s and RF-4s could deliver nuclear weapons, carried usually on the inboard pylons.

Mk 4 rockets. 2.75-inch FFARs with high-explosive, white phosphorus, antiarmor, or fragmentation warheads, typically carried in 19-tube LAU-61 pods and used extensively in Vietnam.

Napalm canisters. BLU-1, BLU-27, and Mk 77 versions, weighing from 500lb to 875lb, were used throughout the Vietnam conflict. Explosivos Alaveses (Expal) BIN-100/-200/-375 were Spanish-produced equivalents.

Leaflet/chaff bomb. The M129E1 fibreglass CBU container was used to distribute propaganda leaflets in Vietnam and to create chaff "corridors" to protect B-52s from enemy radar and SAMs during the Vietnam War. The AN/ALE-38 pod was also used to dispense chaff.

MAIN USAF F-4 PHANTOM II VARIANTS

F-4C

This, the first USAF version, was essentially an F-4B, but within the bounds of commonality some changes were needed for USAF use. The engines (J79-GE-15s) were self-starting, using large Olin Mathiesen MXU-4/A "shotgun" cartridges as an alternative to the MA-1A external pneumatic power source. The APQ-72 radar became the APQ-100, with ground-mapping to assist in ground-attack missions. An upgraded AJB-7 bombing system was added. Later, F-4Cs received a Litton AN/ASN-48 INS. As the USAF initially operated a two-pilot crew concept (rather than the Navy's pilot and radar intercept officer), the rear cockpit was fitted with partial dual controls and had numerous configuration changes. The original Navy probe-and-drogue in-flight refueling system was replaced by a receptacle for the USAF "Flying Boom" system. Beneath the radome, the F-4B's AAA-4 infrared sensor pod was left empty or removed until it was later used for AN/APR-25 RHAW equipment or a strike camera. The aircraft's AN/ASA-32J automatic flight control system (AFCS) comprised an autopilot and stability augmentation function to ease the pilot's load in keeping the aircraft stable without undue control inputs.

Wider main landing-gear wheels were specified for this and all subsequent Phantoms to cope with heavy loads on long, hot runways. Increased tire width (from 7.7 to 11.5 inches) was accommodated by a deeper wheel bay, slightly bulged above and below the wing. A Hydro-Aire antiskid braking system completed a beefy undercarriage installation. The inboard pylons were changed, with an extended curved leading edge to allow more space for wiring in new weapons such as the AGM-12 Bullpup. There were numerous electronic modifications, including an ARW-77 Bullpup missile control system, ASA-32A autopilot, and A24G CADC. However, the changes were not enough to delay production.

Number built: 583. Users: USAF, Spain (1971–79).

In 1976 the Keflavik-based 57th FIS extended its distinctive checkerboard scheme from its F-4Cs' rudders to the whole of the tail during the American Bicentennial year, adding silver-outlined markings for the November 1976 "William Tell" fighter competition. The squadron number appears against a map of Iceland, whose air defense was the unit's responsibility within Air Defense (Atlantic) Command. (USAF)

RF-4C

Structural changes to the F-4C mainly occurred in the nose area to provide suitable accommodation for its cameras and level external surfaces for the optically flat camera windows. In aircraft from serial 69-0376, a more rounded lower nose profile was introduced, and this was retrofitted to selected earlier RF-4Cs. This prevented distortion of the photographic images caused by water vapour in humid conditions gathering around the edges of the forward camera window. Sparrow missile wells were removed and a compartment for photoflash cartridges was installed in both sides of the upper rear fuselage. Each housed a pair of ejectors, one holding 26 110 million candlepower M112 cartridges for low-altitude night photography and the other with ten larger M123 cartridges peaking at 260 million candlepower. In the final batch of 12 RF-4Cs these ejectors were replaced by a single type with 20 M185 cartridges (producing 1 billion candlepower apiece) each side.

The aerodynamic changes made the RF-4C the fastest operational Phantom, capable of 650kt at very low altitude without afterburner and able to be refueled in-flight at over 30,000ft without afterburner, unlike the F-4C/D. The nose housed four primarily photographic sensor types. Three stations were provided, with several options for camera types and positions. In the forward position a KS-87 or KS-72 camera shot from an oblique or vertical viewpoint at adjustable angles. The cameras could be fitted with lens cones of focal lengths between 3 and 18 inches for day photography. Behind this was Station 2, housing either a KA-56 low-altitude panoramic camera or a tri-camera array of three KS-87s, giving vertical views and oblique images from both sides simultaneously. Station 3 at the rear of the bay usually held a KA-55A high-altitude panoramic camera mounted vertically in an LS-58A stabilized mount, or a mapping camera (KC-1 or T-11). The latter could produce up to 460 negatives in 9 x 9-inch format. An AN/AVD-2 laser reconnaissance set was installed here too in the early years. In RF-4Cs up to serial 69-0375 an ejector system, later deleted, was linked to the Station 2 camera and propelled a photo cassette through a small door. The cassette parachuted down, transmitting its position so that data could be recovered and processed before the aircraft landed.

RF-4Cs also had an AN/AAS-18 infrared detecting set, recording a high-resolution film map of the ground, monitored on a rear cockpit TV display. Installed beneath the rear instrument console, it included in-flight processing. Two angular cheek fairings replacing the missile wells on the lower forward fuselage housed the long, rectangular antennas for the Goodyear AN/APQ-102 side-looking radar, which mapped the ground image to each side, detecting any target moving at more than 5kt and recording it on film. APQ-102 saw

C

1. RF-4C-25-MC 65-0841, 38TH TRS, 26TH TRW, RAMSTEIN, WEST GERMANY. NATO EXERCISE ROYAL FLUSH XVI, OCTOBER 1971

2. F-4C-24-MC 64-0859, C12-31 121 ESCUADRON, ALA 12, EDA, TORREJON AB, SPAIN, C. 1975

3. F-4D-31-MC 66-7690, 151ST FIGHTER SQUADRON, 11TH FIGHTER WING, REPUBLIC OF KOREA AIR FORCE, DAEGU AB, SOUTH KOREA, 2006

4. RF-4E-46-MC 69-7499, 348 MIRA, HELLENIC AIR FORCE, LARISSA, GREECE, 2006

1

2

3

4

little operational use and was later replaced by an improved UPD-8 unit in some aircraft.

In the front cockpit the pilot had a radar scope for the AN/APQ-99 (later APQ-172) radar, offering ground mapping, terrain avoidance, and limited air-to-air modes with an optical view-finder in place of the radar screen and weapons control panel of the F-4C. The radar could be operated by either crew member. There was no optical gun/missile sight, apart from a retrofit for some Air National Guard RF-4Cs that were given AIM-9 Sidewinder capability in 1991. In other ways the cockpits resembled the F-4C's, but the AJB-7 bombing computer handled only a nuclear store on a centerline Aero 27A bomb rack.

The RF-4C's lengthy US service period lasted from 1965 to 1995, time for several advanced projects including the General Dynamics HIAC-1 LOROP camera. This 1,000lb unit, in a large G-139 external pod, gave high-resolution images from over 90 miles. Interest in the project switched to the RF-4X and F-4E(S) in the mid-1970s, but it saw limited use by PACAF (Pacific Air Forces) RF-4Cs. TEREC (tactical electronic reconnaissance sensor) or AN/ALQ-125 was developed for the RF-4C by Litton Industries as Pave Onyx. Two antennas detected hostile radar emissions on each side of the aircraft's flight path, presenting this information on a rear cockpit display (prioritized in threat levels as an "order of battle"), and also passing it via datalink to ground sites. Twenty-three 450lb TEREC conversion kits, including digital computers, were supplied for selected RF-4Cs in the late 1970s. Lear Siegler's digital AN/ARN-101(V) DMAS (digital modular avionics suite) was introduced as a major bombing system upgrade for late-production F-4Es but was also planned for 60 RF-4Cs, hugely advancing their navigation capability via updates from the aircraft's radar or LORAN (long-range aid to navigation). It was also linked to 1976 plans for 39 modified RF-4Cs to act as strike control and reconnaissance aircraft, leading a strike package to the target. Associated tests involved the AN/AVQ-26 Pave Tack night-capable laser-targeting pod, which interacted with DMAS.

RF-4Cs were also used by Spain and South Korea.

Camera bay doors on the RF-4 series were made for quick access to the film material in order to hasten processing. To the left in this view is the KS-87B forward oblique station on an RF-4E, with the open KS-56E panoramic station (minus film cassette) to the right. RHAW antennas project from the forward door. (Author)

F-4D

Including more USAF-specified equipment than the F-4C, the F-4D prioritized ground attack and changed the secondary armament from the US Navy's AIM-9 Sidewinder to Hughes' AIM-4D Falcon following "Dancing Falcon" tests at Eglin AFB in 1965. The F-4C's primitive ground-attack capability was enhanced by a new AN/APQ-109A radar including solid-state components and an air-to-ground ranging mode. A wider range of ordnance, including guided air-to-ground weapons such as GBU-9 HOBOS, AGM-12 Bullpup, and AGM-65 Maverick could be carried, and an ASG-22 lead-computing gunsight was added. AIM-9 Sidewinder wiring was restored after the AIM-4D proved unsuitable for close combat use. Nuclear capability was kept, with up to three B61 "special stores" as a typical nuclear alert warload.

USAF F-4D deliveries of 793 aircraft began with a batch for the USAFE (United States Air Forces in Europe)-based 36th TFW in March 1966 and continued into April 1968, with further export production of 32 for Iran until September 1969. It entered combat use with the 555th TFS at Ubon RTAFB in May 1967. Seventy-two had ITT AN/ARN-92 LORAN-D equipment installed, and most of these were also supplied to the 8th TFW at Ubon. LORAN-D, identifiable by a large "towel rack" on the aircraft's back from mid-1969, could be linked to the aircraft's ASN-63 inertial navigation system and bombing computer to calculate the F-4D's position with sufficient accuracy for precision night-time bombing, or for more accurate navigation where the LORAN beacon system was available.

Twenty-two F-4Ds received an important addition from late 1968 in the form of AN/APX-80 Combat Tree. This was able to interrogate the SRO-2 IFF (identification friend or foe) transponders in MiGs, confirming their identity codes at up to 60 miles for attacks with AIM-7 missiles beyond visual range. Wartime rules in Southeast Asia generally required potential enemy "bandits" picked up on radar to be approached for visual identification, thereby losing the advantage of long-range missiles. With Combat Tree this was not required, although officialdom was still reluctant to relax the rules. Similar equipment was later fitted to the majority of USAF F-4Es, and it was used by Iranian F-4s in the Iran–Iraq War. Users: USAF, Iran, Republic of Korea.

F-4E

The addition of an internal 20mm gun was the most important innovation for the F-4E, originally dubbed "F-4E Plus" ("plus gun"). Further improvements and options were introduced during production, including maneuvering slats, Pave Tack, and ARN-101 DMA discussed earlier. The first production configuration for the gun blast diffuser allowed hot gun gases to enter the engine air intakes causing flameouts. The solution was the longer Midas IV diffuser, which directed the gases downwards and sideways, away from the air intakes.

The final ten Production Block 48 aircraft introduced a Northrop AN/ASX-1 TISEO (target identification system, electro-optical) attached to the left wing. Like Combat Tree, it was a way of identifying potentially hostile aircraft that were too distant for the naked eyeball to recognize. TISEO, developed for the F-4E since 1965, was essentially a high-resolution TV camera with two "zoom" settings, linked to the F-4E's radar scope. Capable of resolving a fighter-size image at up to 15 miles, it was combat-tested in 1972 in the Rivet Haste slatted F-4Es sent to battle in the final months of the Vietnam War, where it prevented at least one "blue on blue" loss of another F-4. Although restricted to clear-visibility daylight conditions, TISEO was retained for subsequent production F-4Es from serial 71-0224 onwards.

The analogue APS-107 RHAW set was superseded by the superior Applied Technologies AN/APR-36 and APR-37. This system was later made fully digital as the AN/ALR-46, which was programmable to respond to unforeseen radar threats and could also control external jamming pods like the AN/ALQ-131 in the late 1970s Compass Tie program. These updates deleted the distinctive fin-tip "bullet" fairing and added antennas on the wing-tips, retaining disc antennas on the brake-chute door from the APS-107. Like other F-4 variants, the F-4E received low-voltage formation strip-lights ("slime lights") on the fuselage, tail-fin and wing-tips. Reinforcement straps beneath the wings to help with the extra aerodynamic loads imposed by the slats were replaced by thicker wing skins from Block 48 onwards.

Probably the best known F-4Es were the 18 early-production aircraft allocated to the Thunderbirds Aerial Demonstration Team from April 1969 to November 1973. Several standard camouflaged examples were included for training purposes or to replace the three lost in accidents, but the eight display aircraft bore the team's traditional striking colors and provided thunderously impressive performances. All armament and radars were replaced by ballast, and Sparrow-shaped colored oil smoke tanks were attached. New radios were provided and the engine throttles were tweaked to give full afterburner at only 89 percent military thrust. After 1973 these aircraft were redesignated NF-4Es for test work.

F-4E Kurnass 2000

The introduction of F-15 Eagle and Kfir C1 fighters in 1975 highlighted the need to upgrade Israel's F-4E fleet. Cancellation of the domestic Lavi fighter and the Boeing Super Phantom and lack of funds for an F/A-18 Hornet purchase meant a 15-year life-extension program for the F-4E fleet. New wiring and hydraulics, an Elbit digital avionics computer integrating weapons systems and ACE-3 mission computer, CRTs in both cockpits, a HUD (head-up display), HOTAS (hands-on throttles and stick) throttles, and a new AN/APG-76 radar were the key elements installed as F-4Es arrived

Kurnass 127 (F-4E-43-MC 69-7226) flew with No 119 "Bat" Squadron, with whom it made the IDF/AF's first GBU-8 LGB drop in November 1972, piloted by Aron Ramot and Aharon Katz. Displayed here in No 69 "The Hammers" squadron markings, it has a clutch of TV-guided Mavericks. It was one of four F-4Es converted to interim reconnaissance standard between 1970 and 1975. (via C. Moggeridge)

for PDM (program depot maintenance) from late 1987. Improved navigation and weapon delivery with a more crew-friendly cockpit resulted. F-4E 2020 Terminator was a more sophisticated Kurnass version for the Hellenic Air Force.

F-4EJ

Japan's version of the Phantom in some ways reinstated the aircraft's original naval interceptor guise, including a light gray and white color scheme. After selection of the type in November 1968, the first four F-4Es for Japan came from the McDonnell plant after the first flight on January 14, 1971. Mitsubishi Heavy Industries built 14 more from St Louis-supplied kits in 1971, followed by 125 new-built aircraft. The final aircraft (17-8440), the last of 5,195 Phantoms, emerged from the Japanese factory on May 20, 1981, two years after the last St Louis-built F-4E. Japan's constitution permitted only localized defensive roles, so the AJB-7 bombing computer and in-flight refueling equipment were deleted, though the receptacle for the latter could be retrofitted. F-4EJs had a "hard" (unslatted) wing, an unslotted stabilator, and some Japanese electronics, including an alternative to the AN/APR-35/36 ECM fit, the J/APR-2.

Air defense duties passed to F-15J Eagles from the early 1980s, but their cost prompted a SLEP update initiative to expand the fighter force with "re-lifed" Phantoms from July 1984. The result was 96 extensively rebuilt F-4EJ Kai ("modified") versions, with another 1,500 hours added to their original 3,000 hrs' fatigue life, and advanced, lighter Westinghouse AN/APG-66J pulse-Doppler radars with better "look down" capability to detect targets flying low against a terrain background. Further updates included a Kaiser head-up display, license-built Litton LN-39 laser INS, Japanese-built Tokyo-Keiki APR-6 RHAW system, and new Hazeltine AN/APZ-79A IFF system. The "hard wing" was retained to save cost, but slotted stabilators and the Mitsubishi ASM-1 antishipping missile capability were added.

Another 17 F-4EJs were modified as RF-4EJ Kais to supplement Japan's 14 RF-4EJ reconnaissance Phantoms, although these aircraft retained the F-4E-type nose and gun, carrying their reconnaissance gear in a KS-146B external pod. This comprised a HIAC-1 LOROP camera, Raphael SLAR-2000 sideways-looking radar, and Thales ASTAC electronic intelligence equipment in a separate pod unit. The "Kai" SLEP was included and new AN/APQ-172

306 Hikotai was the last JASDF Phantom squadron to form, establishing itself at Komatsu AB with the 6th Koku-Dan (Air Wing) on June 30, 1981, and the first to receive the F-4EJ Kai in August 1989. Its golden eagle ("inuwashi") squadron badge, also the insignia of the local Ishikawa prefecture, was a recognition that real golden eagles soared around the mountains nearby. (Author's collection)

radars were installed. "Kai" aircraft are identifiable by larger UHF antennas on their spines and four thin reinforcing strips attached to their radomes. Confusingly, several standard RF-4EJs also received the "Kai" appellation when they too received SLEP updates, including APQ-172 radar. Japan's original 14 RF-4EJs were built to the same standard as Luftwaffe RF-4Es.

F-4E(S) Tsalam Shablul (Snail)

Originally intended for the Martin RB-57F high-altitude reconnaissance aircraft, the General Dynamics HIAC-1 LOROP camera was developed and lightened from 3,500lb to 1,500lb. It then fitted the G-139 "Miflas" pod, which, with other sensors added, hung on an F-4's centerline. Tests in an RF-4C in Project Peace Eagle flights around North Korea's borders showed that its drag reduced the Phantom's speed and altitude to the point where the HIAC-1's high resolution was reduced. Attention then turned to a much-modified F-4E, the F-4X/RF-4X, with revised Mach 3.2 air intakes and two 2,500-gallon water tanks in aerodynamic fairings on the upper fuselage. Water was injected into the air intakes, cooling the airflow enough to allow increased engine speed, more prolonged afterburner use and sustained Mach 2.4 cruise speeds. The HIAC-1 camera was installed in a revised nose, replacing the radar and gun. Israel bought into the project and IDF/AF F-4E 69-7576 was used for a mock-up of the modifications. In the USA it was felt that this potentially outstanding Phantom version threatened sales of the F-15 Eagle. Delays prompted Israel to investigate a simpler F-4E version, the F-4E(S) with nose-mounted LOROP (disguised by a painted-on "radome") and digital camera controls in the rear cockpit. Only three of these "Peace Jack" conversions were funded, entering service in May 1976. HIAC-1 could be exchanged for a KA-801 panoramic camera or HR-308T diagonal-photographic camera. The F-4(S) examples were 69-7567/490, 69-7570/492 (a former MiG-killer), and 69-7576/493. They were retired in May 2004.

RF-4E

This was basically an F-4E with an RF-4C reconnaissance nose, slatted stabilator, and "hard" wing. In May 1968 Germany ordered 88 RF-4Es as RF-104G Starfighter replacements, with USAF serials 69-7448 to 69-7535 and Luftwaffe codes 35+01 to 35+88. They were upgraded from 1979 to add 5,000lb of conventional ordnance to their recce capability, and an AN/APD-11 SLAR could be carried in a centerline pod instead of the internal SLAR. Datalink and film cassette ejection were carried over from the RF-4C, and AN/ALE-chaff dispensers were attached to the wing pylons. Israel ordered six

D

1. F-4G-42-MC 69-0244 "NIGHT STALKER," 23RD TFS, 7440TH CW, SHEIKH ISA AB, BAHRAIN, FEBRUARY 1991

2. F-4E-51-MC 71-1099 3-6549, 61ST TFS, ISLAMIC REPUBLIC OF IRAN AIR FORCE, TFB.6 BUSHEHR AB, IRAN, 2009

3. F-4EJ 67-8386, 302ND HIKOTAI, SOUTHWEST COMPOSITE WING, JAPAN AIR SELF-DEFENSE FORCE, NAHA, OKINAWA, 1993

4. F-4E-35-MC 67-0301, 112 FILO, 1ST TACTICAL AIR FORCE, TURK HAVA KUVVETLERI, ESKISEHIR AB, TURKEY, 1988

RF-4E-45-MCs in July 1968, specifying secondary tactical weapons capability including inboard MAU-12 pylons for AIM-9 Sidewinders or SUU-23 gun-pods and air-to-ground ordnance. RF-4Es arrived from February 1971, supplemented by four F-4Es locally modified to carry a downward-pointing KS-87 camera instead of the internal gun. Israel's RF-4Es often used their AN/APQ-99 radar's ground-mapping facility for low-altitude penetration flights. Camera equipment on their standard RF-4Es comprised KS-87, KA-116, and Zeiss RMK-A 15/23 units. Turkish RF-4Es also used the KS-87 but with KA-56 vertical low-altitude panoramic cameras and Elbit-Elop video cameras in the nose. They could use the G-139 LOROP pod and their rear cockpits were updated with a multi-function display (MFD) unit. Japan received 14 St Louis-built RF-4Es, lacking only standard RHAW systems, between November 1974 and June 1975.

QF-4E/G/RF-4C

The USAF engaged Tracor Flight Systems (later BAE Systems) in 1992 to convert surplus F-4s into full scale aerial targets, beginning with the recently stored F-4Gs. When they were used up by 2002 low-hours, ARN-101/DMAS F-4Es were processed up to summer 2008 and RF-4Cs from April 1997, with RF-4C 68-0609 as the last of 318 QF-4s. Delivered to the 82nd Aerial Target Squadron at Tyndall AFB, Florida, the QF-4s initially fly manned chase or test flights but eventually join the "Death Row" NULLO (not under live local operator) unmanned target line-up. Ejection seats and other equipment are then removed. Fitted with an AFCS and command/telemetry (CTS) gear, the aircraft become targets for armament tests and fighter-training missile shoots, often using unarmed missiles to increase drone life. Hits and misses are recorded by an electronic scoring system, and a self-destruct charge completes the job if the drone is unsafe for return to base. NULLO operations began in May 1995, and in 2011 the 82nd ATRS added target-banner towing to its duties, replacing Lear jets. In 2004 a few QF-4Es were repainted as the Heritage Flight for public demonstrations. These QF-4s perform normal flight duties and are eventually destined for NULLO expenditure.

F-4F

In 1971 West Germany required an F-104 Starfighter replacement that would fill the gap while the Panavia Tornado was developed. A cheaper version of the F-4 without the second cockpit and Sparrow capability and using more basic avionics seemed appropriate. McDonnell had explored the possibilities of an exportable single-seat F-4E to rival Northrop's F-5E Tiger in the competition for an Advanced International Fighter (IFX). It soon became clear to the German Department of Defense that development of a single-seater F-4E(F) for their own purposes would be prohibitively expensive, so a stock F-4E, modified with leading-edge slats and the deletion of the AIM-7, slotted stabilator, in-flight refueling, and seventh fuel tank, and equipped with a simplified AN/APQ-120(V)5 radar, was chosen. The deleted equipment reduced overall weight by 3,300lb.

An order for 175 Peace Rhine F-4Fs (US serials 72-1111 to 72-1285) was placed in August 1971, with some airframe parts contracted out to German industry. The engines were built by Motoren und Turbinen Union (MTU), Munich as J79-MTU-17As, using that company's experience in manufacturing similar J79s for the F-104G. The first F-4F flew on March 18, 1973 and the first 12 aircraft were used for training JG (Jagdgeschwader) 71 "Richthofen" Luftwaffe crews at George AFB under the auspices of the 35th TFW. The F-4F's reduced armament of four AIM-9s and gun limited its air-to-air engagement potential to tail-chase interceptions, and in 1975 agreement was reached with the US Government to add air-to-ground capability and make the F-4F compatible with USAFE Phantoms and NATO stores, including BL755 CBU and MATRA retarded bombs. F-4Fs equipped two ground-attack wings and two interceptor wings. In the Peace Rhine program from 1980 to 1984 MBB/DASA in Germany installed LRU-1 weapons computers, including a signal condition converter to digitize its data. Litton produced an AN/ALR-68 RHAW system for the F-4F and the missile rails were changed from Aero 3Bs to LAU-7A/5 (FRG) models to accept the much improved AIM-9L Sidewinder. ALE-40 chaff dispensers were included in the upgrade, but Sparrow capability was still omitted. F-4Fs received their new air-to-air Norm 81 A/B camouflage scheme, replacing the earlier green "splinter" pattern. The original Royal Jet 600-gallon centerline fuel tank was replaced by the F-15-type HPC unit, which is more resistant to "g."

Peace Rhine F-4Fs remained in service after the introduction of the Tornado, but the development of the Eurofighter for air defense duties was very protracted and a further upgrade program was therefore planned for the F-4F, extending its service life to 2013. A three-stage improved combat efficiency (ICE, known to some as "in-cockpit entertainment") initiative, run by EADS (European Aeronautical Defence and Space Company), extended airframe life for up to 10,000 hours through improved inspection and repair. The second stage provided a Honeywell H-423 laser INS and GEC Marconi CPU-143/A digital air data computer, together with a MIL STD 1553B digital databus. Forty-three F-4Fs went through the first two stages only from 1989, and they were known as ICE/KWS-Luftangriffsvarianten (or KWS-LA), optimized for ground attack. Although they also received a new Norm 90J three-tone gray air superiority paint scheme, they retained APQ-120 radars with black radomes. In the third stage of ICE, 110 F-4F KWS-Luftverteidigung (or FV) fighters received a major air combat improvement via the Hughes/Raytheon AIM-120 AMRAAM air-to-air missile and multi-mode APG-65 radar, license-built in Germany by Bodensee Geraet Technik and originally specified for the F/A-18 Hornet. F-4Fs thereby had the beyond-visual-range punch that they had lacked since their introduction. These aircraft are visually identified by their light gray Marion Composites radomes, which are very slightly wider than previous F-4E/F radomes. As a cost-saver the Phantom's distinctive smoke-trail was not among the ICE improvements. The final upgraded F-4F was completed in January 1997.

F-4G

The Wild Weasel V F-4G program used 134 F-4Es with 1969 serial numbers and reused a designation that had previously applied to a dozen datalink-modified F-4Bs. The first aircraft took to the air on December 6, 1975. To conduct its specialized SEAD activities, the F-4E airframe had to accommodate over 50 ECM antennas and an AN/APR-38 (later APR-47 for Wild Weasel VI) Pave Strike radar and missile detection and launch homing system, housed in the space vacated by the Vulcan cannon and requiring 25 line-replaceable units (LRUs) in all. The revised gun "gondola" had three low-band antennas on each side and high/mid-band antennas in an extended bullet fairing on the tail-fin's tip and on its leading edge. In the rear cockpit, major alterations to the front instrument panels provided the weapons systems operator (WSO, or "Bear") with large, new CRT screens centered on a 10-inch plan position indicator (PPI) to monitor and prioritize threat radars and manage the AGM-45C Shrike, AGM-78D Standard ARM, or AGM-88 HARM missiles. Although these revisions completely blocked the Bear's forward vision, a set of flying controls was retained. The PPI was repeated in the front cockpit and threats were presented on the pilot's LCOSS "gunsight." AGM-65 Maverick could be carried as well as free-fall ordnance.

The addition of the ARN-101 digital modular avionics suite from 1987 required a 36-button keypad in the rear cockpit. Air-to-air missiles were retained, including just two AIM-7Fs, as the forward wells were "dearmed" to allow for AN/ALQ-119 or ALQ-131 (V) ECM pods to be carried. The centerline stores position was adapted for the 6g F-15 fuel tank. In the mid-1980s a performance update program (PUP) replaced the APR-38 RHAW

To improve pilot's limited forward vision, a one-piece windshield was tested. The new installation, including a wider, stronger titanium frame, also doubled as bird-strike protection. About 20 F-4E, F-4G, and RF-4C windshields were replaced, including that of F-4E-40-MC 68-0473 of 7ci, Turkish AF still displaying its previous 110th TFS, Missouri ANG crew chief's name. (Author)

with the far more advanced APR-47, giving vastly increased memory, speed, and threat-processing power. It was linked to a bulky video tape recorder near the pilot's right arm, which recorded all information from the main radar scope. Protection from heatseeking missiles came from an AN/ALE-40 dispenser set, emitting RR-170A/AL chaff cartridges or MJU-7/B infrared flares from locations on both sides of the inboard weapons pylons.

F-4 Dimensions					
	Wingspan	Wingspan folded	Length	Height	Wing area
F-4C/D	38ft 5in.	27ft 7in	58ft 3in.	16ft 6in.	530sqft
RF-4C	38ft 5in.	27ft 7in	62ft 11in.	16ft 6in.	530sqft
F-4E	38ft 5in.	27ft 7in	62ft 11in.	16ft 6in.	530sqft
RF-4E	38ft 5in.	27ft 7in	63ft	16ft 6in.	530sqft
F-4G	38ft 5in.	27ft 7in	63ft	16ft 6in.	530sqft

Weights (lb), typical				
	Empty (basic)	Combat	Max take-off**	Landing
F-4C	28,890	38,606	59,689	34,878*
RF-4C	29,741	40,267	58,000	33,598
F-4D	29,224	38,706	59,483	35,195*
F-4E	31,853	41,487	61,795	36,080*
RF-4E	31,110	41,000	52,836	35,000
F-4F	30,328	41,000	61,000	36,000
F-4G	33,000	41,500	61,795	36,690

*after ground attack sortie.

** Normal maximum was 58,000lb. Abnormal tire wear was likely above this weight.

Performance (speed in mph, ceiling in ft, distances in miles)				
	Speed (sea level / 40,000 / cruise)	Ceiling (max / combat)	Combat radius	Ferry range
F-4C	826 / 1,433 / 587	55,600 / 24,450*	285*	1,926
RF-4C	834 / 1,459 / 587	59,400 / –	673**	1,750
F-4D	826 / 1,432 / 587	55,850 / 24,550*	266*	1,844
F-4E/F	914 / 1,430 / 585	59,600 / 28,100*	266*	1,885
RF-4E	898 / 1,485 / 587	62,250 / –	673**	1,885
F-4G	910 / 1,472 / 585	58,750 / 28,000	422	1,615

* with two 370-gallon external tanks, four AIM-7s and 11 M117 bombs.

** high-altitude mission with three external tanks.

N.B. All performance figures vary depending on factors such as mission type, atmospheric conditions, and the age of the aircraft.

OPERATIONAL HISTORY

United States Air Force

Southeast Asia

Although the Phantom II was flown by many air forces in diverse roles, the basic "crew concept" was generally much the same. The front-seater was usually the aircraft commander, responsible for flying the aircraft and briefing with his back-seater on the mission to ensure an effective division of responsibilities. He ensured that the numerous prescriptive checklists were followed, from preflight inspection to engine shutdown. The second crewman handled navigation, operating radar, reconnaissance or weapons controls as required, and monitored instruments, particularly during climb or dive

maneuvers. Crucially, he was also a second pair of eyes to detect threats from the air or ground and deal with in-flight emergencies when his access to the numerous circuitbreakers in the rear cockpit could save a situation. TAC fighter tactics evolved from Korean-era, rigid four-ship flights, where only the two flight leaders were "shooters," to a more flexible, US Navy-type approach. MiG-killer Phil Handley:

> When I flew the F-86 Sabre, "Fluid Four" was the way to go when altitude was king and you tried to get as high as possible. When you move the fight down into the dense air of 15–20,000ft and turns are made with relatively high g-force, the wingman doesn't have a chance during a patrol turn and becomes MiG bait.

Phil was one of the first to employ "Fluid Two," mutually supporting flights of paired F-4s.

For many first-generation USAF Phantom pilots, who were mainly from single-seat fighter squadrons, the idea of working with a second crew member was awkward. Accustomed to managing the aircraft and its radar and weapons single-handedly, some regarded the back-seater as "talking ballast," who would merely interfere with the front-seater's command. Unlike the US Navy's pilot-plus-radar intercept officer team, the USAF initially classed both crew members as pilots, each with a set of controls. By 1969 experience brought a change and the "guy in back" ("GIB") became a weapon systems operator (WSO). It took time to develop the effective team cockpit drills that have been used and adapted by most air forces using the Phantom II. Although the Hellenic, Japanese, and Iranian Air Forces preferred the two-pilot arrangement, the teamwork idea still applied.

Vietnam War pressure lent urgency to TAC's F-4 crew training program at McDill AFB, Florida (later at Davis-Monthan AFB, Arizona), where the 4453rd CCTW moved in July 1964. After initial training with the 4453rd CCTW, the first operational USAF Phantom II wing, the 12th TFW, was ready to deploy to Cam Ranh Bay, South Vietnam by November 8, 1965, and it flew combat operations for six years. The 15th TFW also exchanged its Republic F-84Fs for F-4Cs at McDill from May 1964 and detached squadrons to Cam Ranh Bay and to Ubon RTAFB, Thailand in 1965, where its 45th TFS scored the first USAF Phantom MiG kills on July 10. F-4Cs replaced F-100 Super Sabres as the primary escort fighter over North Vietnam, and they had destroyed 42 MiG-17 and MiG-21 adversaries by June 5, 1967, losing only five F-4Cs to MiGs. In May 1967 F-4Ds arrived at Ubon and shot down another 17 MiGs by the end of the Operation *Rolling Thunder* campaign, despite being hampered by their problematic AIM-4 Falcon armament.

Although MiGs were a real threat to the large strike packages attacking North Vietnam, they were used sparingly. F-4C/D MiGCAPs usually required two flights of four Phantom IIs (from around 24 aircraft per squadron) flying "shotgun" behind the strikers but within the ECM cover provided after mid-1967 by jamming pods. As Col Robin Olds, commanding the 8th TFW from September 30, 1966 described it, the F-4s were

part of a 28 to 32 aircraft strike force which roars in at 520 to 560kt at 13,000 to 17,000ft, strikes one to three closely spaced targets with all the aircraft on and off the target in less than a minute and then withdraws in a deceptively well-ordered gaggle at up to 600kt until out of the high-threat area.

The 12th TFW at Cam Ranh Bay used "X" codes from December 1966 to March 1970, XN indicating the 559th TFS, "blue" squadron. F-4C-23-MC 64-0750 taxis out with ordnance, including a 20mm SUU-16/A gun-pod, for one of the ground-attack missions that constituted almost all the wing's wartime "business." (via Norman Taylor)

Col Robin Olds, a leader who inspired genuine devotion from his men, used his long fighter experience to devise new tactics for the 8th TFW and led by example. F-4C-24-MC, 64-0829 "Scat XXVII" continued a series of his fighters beginning with "Scat II," a WWII P-38 named after his room-mate, "Scat" Davis, in 1943. This F-4C, displaying the 433rd TFS "Satan's Angels" insignia, was used for two of his MiG kills (on May 20, 1967), attacks on the Paul Doumer Bridge and Thai Nguyen steel mill, and for his final combat mission. (USAF)

The F-4D entered combat in May 1967, joined in November 1968 by the F-4E. Bob Jasperson recalled: "At Da Nang AB it was not unusual to have the numbers 1 and 3 in a flight in F-4Es and the wingmen in F-4Ds. At Korat RTAFB the four-ship would all be the same model, but they would assign the F-4Es for escort and MiGCAP and the F-4Ds for bombing missions." This F-4D-42-MC, 66-8784, has "Assam Dragons. 25th Tac Ftr Sqn" on its yellow canopy sills. (Al Piccirillo via Norman Taylor)

As Phantoms gradually took over the strike role from F-105s, they could also use their missiles or guns for self-defense after dropping ordnance.

MiGCAP flights were sometimes doubled for the larger airstrikes of Operation *Linebacker II* in 1972, and additional F-4D/E flights joined four F-105Gs on hazardous SEAD flak-suppressing missions with bombs and CBU. Others comprised "chaffing" flights: flying in-line abreast, straight and level, dropping chaff corridors to protect the bombers while making ideal targets for AAA and SAMs themselves. MiG killer Fred Sheffler recalled this as "one very undesirable mission." Chaffing also required an F-4 escort to ward off MiGs. Prestrike weather reconnaissance and poststrike bomb-damage assessment were provided by RF-4C Phantoms. Many pilots flew these missions without seeing MiGs and regarded AAA or SAMs as much worse threats, but when the MiGCAP flights got lucky they could inflict real damage on the VPAF (Vietnamese Peoples' Air Force) fighters. Operation *Bolo* on January 2, 1967 was one of the best days. MiG-21s were lured into a trap by Col Olds' F-4Cs posing as F-105 bombers and seven were shot down without loss, grounding the small MiG-21 force for three months. Lts Ralph Wetterhahn and Terry Sharp in F-4C 63-7589 took the first MiG-21, firing two AIM-7Es.

> The first was felt to launch, but was not observed. The second launched and it appeared just left of the radome. It guided up to the MiG-21 (range 1.5–2 miles) and impacted just forward of the stabilizer. A red fireball appeared and the MiG-21 flew through it, continued on for an instant and then swapped ends, shedding large portions of the aft section. The aircraft went into a flat spin and rotated slowly until it disappeared into the clouds.

The AIM-7 was poorly suited to most of the engagements over Vietnam and pilots often resorted to the close-in Sidewinder with better results. MiG-killer John Markle:

> We were trained to fire two Sparrows against each target. The reliability of the weapon was built into our training: fire two, with a 50 percent probability [of a successful launch].

While MiGCAP duties at Ubon became the specialty of the 555th TFS, the 8th TFW's 497th TFS became the "Night Owl" unit, mainly flying demanding nocturnal strikes over Laos and North Vietnam and bombing under the light of flares. The F-4C had no specialized bombing equipment for this potentially disorientating task, but enemy supply lines, which moved at night, were often disrupted. Ubon's 422nd TFS took the early evening strike slots. The 12th TFW's four squadrons were installed at Cam Ranh Air Base ("CRAB") from November 1965, led by Col Levi R. Chase, a veteran of both WWII and Korean fighter operations, like many early F-4 commanders. Their missions were interdiction and close support for troops in South Vietnam and Laos, with some tedious escort flights over the Gulf of Tonkin to protect reconnaissance aircraft. By June 1966 Lt Jackson Shockley had flown the wing's 5,000th sortie, the 558th TFS had fired off 1.4 million rounds of 20mm gun-pod ammunition, and Capt Robert Street had made the first wheels-up F-4C landing, setting his jet down on its wing-tank "pontoons" almost intact at Bien Hoa.

Korat RTAFB exchanged its F-105Ds for F-4Es from May 1969, flying CAP and strike missions mainly over North Vietnam where ten MiGs were "scored" up to December 1975. At Da Nang AB, after a brief assignment to Phan Rang AB, the 366th TFW under Col Allan Rankin ran three F-4C units, which focussed on in-country close support but also shared the escort missions over North Vietnam, where they destroyed 17 MiGs, four of them with the SUU-16/A gun-pod. In January 1967 they also introduced the system of two-letter aircraft codes that soon became standard, though their system coded individual aircraft rather than squadrons. The 460th TRW at the overcrowded Tan Son Nhut AB, which replaced its RF-101C Voodoos with two squadrons of RF-4Cs from October 1965, was responsible for all reconnaissance duties in Southeast Asia, using over 200 aircraft of various types. It was partnered by the 432nd TRW at Udorn RTAFB from October 1966, using two RF-4C squadrons. They continued to fly hazardous yet essential single-aircraft daytime photo runs and nocturnal infrared sorties, relying on speed and agility to defeat defensive forces that often knew when and where they would appear. Eighty-three RF-4Cs and 65 crew members were lost, almost half over North Vietnam.

The end of *Rolling Thunder* and the drawdown of US forces in Southeast Asia from late 1969 reduced the 12th TFW to two squadrons, relocated at Phu Cat AB, while the 366th TFW hosted two F-4E squadrons from 1969 alongside two F-4D units before being reassigned to Takhli RTAFB in 1972. In Thailand

LEFT The 480th TFS moved to Phu Cat AB with the 37th TFW in April 1969 and HK codes. F-4D-29-MC 66-7501 was a MiG-killer, downing a MiG-21 on October 13, 1971 with a 432nd TRW crew, Lt Col Curtis Westphal and Capt Jeff Feinstein. It was lost on November 20, 1972 after control failure, with another crew of double MiG-killers (Capt Calvin Tibbett and 1Lt William Hargrove) aboard. (via Norman Taylor)

RIGHT F-4E-35-MC 67-0296 of the 469th TFS, 388th TFW was part of BASS escort flight near Hanoi on July 5, 1972. The F-4Es were jumped by MiG-21PFMs and this aircraft, BASS 02 with Capt William Spencer and 1Lt Brian Seek, was shot down. Moments later, BASS 04 (67-0339 with Major Bill Elander and 1Lt Don Logan – later a prolific author) was also hit. All four USAF crew members became prisoners of war. (via Norman Taylor)

the 8th TFW moved its MiG-killing 555th TFS to the 432nd TRW in 1968 and hosted successive temporary deployments by eight US-based F-4E units to boost numbers during the 1972 *Linebacker* campaign, as did the expanded, diverse 432nd TRW, which remained active at Udorn (as the 432nd TFW) until June 1975. Other PACAF F-4 wings were also available for temporary war service, including the 18th TFW at Kadena AB, Okinawa and the 405th TFW at Clark AFB, Philippines. The latter was replaced by the 3rd TFW in 1974 operating F-4E/Gs until 1991. In Japan the 475th TFW had F-4C/Ds at Misawa AB from 1968 to 1971 before becoming a re-formed 3rd TFW at Kunsan, South Korea, where it flew air defense missions with the 51st Air Base Wing's F-4Es from Osan.

CONUS (continental US) and USAFE units

A third South Korean-based wing, the 54th TFW, also flew F-4Es briefly from Kunsan AB in 1970, with squadrons borrowed from US-based wings. The 4th TFW at Seymour-Johnson AB, one of the longest-serving F-4 units (1967–88),

rotated squadrons through both Kunsan and Ubon RTAFB during the war, as did the 33rd TFW from Eglin AFB, Florida, which specialized in forming F-4 squadrons for wartime deployment. Crested Cap USAFE deployments were also made by 4th TFW F-4Es in the 1970s. Other CONUS wings including the 1st TFW, 21st CW/TFW, 31st TFW, 35th TFW, and 56th TFW concentrated on US-based air defense or training, although the latter was the specialism of the 56th, 57th, and 58th tactical training wings. Tactical reconnaissance was the preserve of two RF-4C units, the 67th TRW at Bergstrom AFB and the 363rd TRW at Shaw AFB, South Carolina. Two F-4C/E units, the 57th FIS defending Iceland and the 32nd TFS on interception duties at Soesterberg, Holland, operated as single squadrons without a "parent" wing.

The 49th TFW was US-based at Holloman AFB, New Mexico but committed also to NATO, making frequent Reforger rapid deployments to German bases. It reinforced regular USAFE F-4 wings including the West German-based 36th TFW at Bitburg, 52nd TFW at Spangdahlem AB, 50th TFW at Hahn AB, and 86th TFW at Zweibrucken (before moving to

An AGM-88A HARM missile takes flight from this F-4G-43-MC, 69-7231 in 35th TFW markings. F-4 Weasel pilots had a "pinky switch" to select heat-seeking missiles, radar AIM-7 missiles, or a gun-pod in addition to the controls for antiradiation missiles or free-fall ordnance. Jim Hendrickson flew both F-4Es and F-4Gs, finding the latter to have "the same airframe, less space, less visibility, more electronic toys and a heck of a lot more to do." (USAF)

The 4th TFW at Seymour Johnson AFB, North Carolina was one of the largest TAC F-4 operators, partly because it was tasked with providing short-notice reinforcement deployments worldwide. The entire wing flew to Kunsan, South Korea for the 1968 Pueblo Crisis, sent squadrons with the first slatted F-4Es to Thailand for Operation *Linebacker*, and made many Crested Cap NATO deployments. (USAF)

Ramstein AB), all poised to hold back an Eastern Bloc invasion with nuclear or conventional ordnance or to intercept intruders. Even the advanced F-4E had difficulties with the latter, as Major Jim Chamberlain, flying F-4Es with the 496th TFS, 50th TFW in 1970, recalled:

> One of the most likely avenues of attack was low level, and in that area we were severely limited. The APQ-120 radar of the F-4E was far better than the APQ-109 of the F-4D but still not very good close to the ground. Nor did we practice low-level intercepts. All we could do was use the look-up or look-down methods to detect the target with the radar side-lobes, and that resulted in the radar breaking lock to the ground.

From April 1965, USAFE tactical recce fell to the RF-4Cs of the 26th TRW (initially at Ramstein AB and later, exchanging with the 86th TFW, at Zweibrucken) and until 1987 to the RAF Alconbury, UK-based 10th TRW, which also took on the 23rd TRS, displaced from Toul-Rosières in France by General de Gaulle's expulsion of US units. The British-based strike Phantom units, the 48th TFW at RAF Lakenheath and 81st TFW at RAF Bentwaters/Woodbridge, flew F-4C/Ds before converting to the GD F-111 Aardvark. The first 81st TFW F-4C arrived on October 4, 1965, and up to 12 could be on nuclear alert at times of particular tension, armed from the NATO "Cube" nuclear Weapons Storage Area on the base's "Hot Row." Every year half of each of the three squadrons made 30-day deployments quarterly to Wheelus AB near Tripoli for weapons practise on the vast Sahara ranges. With flight-line temperatures approaching 150 degrees Fahrenheit and sandstorms roaring in from the desert, the only escape was to the "Halfway House" snack bar on the extensive beach. Between 1966 and 1967 many 81st TFW personnel were reassigned to Southeast Asian bases because of shortages there. The war also caused an acute shortage of KC-135 tankers, requiring 7,000 "Creek Party" sorties by piston-engined ANG KC-97s between 1970 and 1977. A single USAFE F-4 wing in Spain, the 401st TFW at Torrejon AB, initially converted to the F-4E, but then reverted to F-4Cs from the 81st TFW, with F-4Ds following in 1978.

E   **VIETNAM, NOVEMBER 1967**

On November 6, 1967, Capt Darrell D. Simmons and 1Lt George H. McKinney Jr were flying F-4D-30-MC 66-7601 from the 435th TFS, 8th TFW as part of a MiGCAP for an F-105 Thunderchief strike. They had just shot down a MiG-17 that was threatening the F-105s and five minutes later they dived to pursue and shoot down a second MiG, also with their SUU-23/A 20mm gun-pod. 1Lt McKinney, 66-7601 and its gun-pod scored another MiG-17 on December 19 with Major Joseph Moore as "nose gunner".

Some F-4s appeared with white maintenance stencilling in the 1970s, though rules about colors for NATO and other emergency or ground handling placards still applied. The 49th TFW wore "HO" (for Holloman AFB, New Mexico) codes for five years between its 1972 Southeast Asia deployment and conversion to the F-15 Eagle. From 1968 it made many NATO Reforger rapid deployment exercises to Germany. (USAF via M. Charlton)

The last war for USAF Phantom IIs was fought 26 years after their first. In January 1991 several converted Vietnam-veteran F-4Es reappeared in battle among 61 F-4G Wild Weasels with the 35th TFW (Provisional) at Sheik Isa AB, Bahrain and the 7440th CW "Superwing" at Incirlik AB, Turkey to provide SEAD assets for the Gulf War. Drawing aircraft from the 35th and 52nd TFWs respectively, these two forces were in the opening onslaught involving 2,000 aircraft on the first night of Operation *Desert Storm*. Vietnam experience had shown all too vividly how SAMs could destroy aircraft at anything above 300ft altitude, or at least force the attackers down into light AAA range, usually after jettisoning their ordnance to achieve maneuverability. In Iraq the coalition forces faced at least 400 batteries of SAMs, including Vietnam-era SA-2s and ten far more sophisticated types, totaling 16,000 missiles, plus over 7,000 portable infrared, short-range weapons. A massive early-warning network and a force of 700 defending fighters in a complex command and control system completed this daunting scenario. On the night of January 16/17, 1991 F-4Gs of the 81st and 561st TFS were a vital part of a carefully choreographed USAF SEAD assault also involving BQM-74C decoy drones to make enemy radars switch on and reveal their locations, and EF-111A Raven and EC-130H electronic warfare aircraft. F-4Gs smashed SAM sites in Kuwait and around Baghdad, firing 200 AGM-88 HARMs (the 35th TFW eventually fired 1,100) in the first 24 hours of the campaign. With up to six Weasels per mission, SEAD was provided for strike formations of B-52s, F-111s, and F-16s, with hunter-killer F-16Cs carrying bombs and CBU following up for DEAD (destruction of enemy air defenses). As the campaign progressed, Maverick, Shrike, and CBU-89 were also employed in follow-up F-4G missions up to April 1991, when the Weasels went home. No coalition aircraft were lost while the Weasels were on patrol, and only one F-4G was

The 160th TRS, 187th TRG, Alabama ANG sent a team of RF-4Cs to participate in the NATO 1980 Best Focus tactical air reconnaissance meet at Eggebeck, Germany. Several ANG RF-4C squadrons displayed their identities vertically on the rudder at that time. (Author's collection)

lost (to fuel starvation) in 2,678 sorties against intense opposition. By April 113 SAM sites were knocked out, with nine crews responsible for five or more sites and Capt Vinnie Quinn with Major Ken Spaar claiming 12. The 81st TFS destroyed 142 radar sites in all, mainly with the HARM, which, as Capt "Spike" Benyshek described it, moved so fast that "usually, the pilot's first view of the missile is when it is already 1,000ft in front of the aircraft." Although it was announced that F-4Gs would leave active duty by the end of 1992, the demands of *Southern Watch* and *Provide Comfort* operations to keep the pressure on Saddam Hussein delayed the retirement of 561st FS F-4Gs until March 22, 1996.

ANG and AFRES

The last front-line F-4Gs in Saudi Arabia and Turkey were joined by others that had been passed to the 190th FS, Idaho ANG, in 1992. This unit continued to fly Weasels until December 1995 and SEAD duties gradually passed to the arguably less capable F-16CJ. Also providing a vital part of the limited tactical reconnaissance force during the Gulf War were RF-4Cs of the Alabama and Nevada ANG, which demonstrated that the Phantom's surveillance capability, including the LOROP cameras of the former unit, were a crucial factor in the campaign. They detected enemy units in Kuwait, provided valuable daylight imagery of targets in the Baghdad area, and (with other RF-4Cs detached from the 26th and 67th TRWs) took part in the endless search for Saddam's Scud missile launchers.

The "TX" tailcodes and tail-flash of F-4D-32-MC 66-8740 indicate its Texas home at Bergtrom AFB where this Air Force Reserve unit flew F-4D/Es for ten years from 1981. It has the revised antennas ("Herpes" mod) of the Bendix AN/ALR-69(V)2 RHAW gear on the pod under its radome and an AVQ-23 Pave Spike unit in a forward Sparrow well. (USAF)

The Alabama ANG was the first to fly Phantoms when RF-4Cs for its 106th TFS "Recce Rebels" began to arrive in February 1971. For Gulf operations in 1990, six RF-4Cs made the 8,000-mile transit to Abu Dhabi with 16 in-flight refuelings. The unit made the RF-4C's last operational flight in May 1995. Nine other ANG squadrons had RF-4Cs, including another Alabama unit, the 160th TRS, which transitioned to the F-4D in 1983 after 12 years of recce Phantoms. As F-4Cs were replaced in active squadrons, they moved in large numbers to 14 ANG squadrons between 1972 and 1989. F-4Ds were

also reassigned to 14 units, ten of which had not flown F-4Cs previously, and four of the F-4C squadrons upgraded to F-4Es from 1985 until their F-4E usage ended in 1991. The fifth, the 141st TFS, New Jersey ANG, had previously flown F-4Ds. The last F-4C unit was the 114th TFTS, Oregon ANG, in 1989, having served as a training unit for ANG Phantom II units. All ANG F-4s had been replaced by the end of 1996.

In February 1971 the 106th TRS "Recce Rebels" from Birmingham, Alabama was the first of nine ANG units to fly the RF-4C. It deployed eight BH-coded, LOROP-capable aircraft to Sheikh Isa AB, Bahrain in August 1990 with the 35th TFW(P), including 64-1047 "Scud Seeker," seen here with an AN/ALQ-131 ECM pod. They flew 412 valuable sorties, searching out Iraqi missiles and troops and providing BDA. (USAF)

ANG schedules often included foreign deployments, which were invariably conducted with great efficiency by highly experienced air and ground crews. California's 194th FIS took on air defense at Ramstein AB, Germany in 1986 as well as maintaining an interception role at George AFB. Coronet exercises took Arkansas ANG F-4Cs to Turkey and Panama between 1981 and 1986 and California's other F-4 unit to Spain in 1986. From Hawaii the 199th TFS deployed to Japan and the Philippines several times, and the 113rd TFS from Terre Haute, Indiana flew its F-4Cs to a 1978 Coronet Quail reinforcement in Italy. The USAF's Total Force concept brought fighter units to the USAF Reserve from 1972 and the 89th TFS was the first F-4C unit in 1978, converting to F-4Ds in 1982 as one of six units with that model. Two squadrons, the 457th TFS "Texas Humpbacks" and the 704th TFS (also from Texas), went on to fly F-4Es until 1991.

Royal Australian Air Force

When the RAAF ordered General Dynamics F-111Cs for delivery in 1967 it was assumed that the resident Canberra bombers would last until that time. The F-111Cs were actually six years late arriving, and an interim deal for 24 leased F-4E Phantoms was offered. They equipped numbers 1 and 6 squadrons of No 82 (Bomber) Wing at Amberley from September 1970. They were newly built, hard-wing F-4E-43-MCs provided through the Peace Reef program. Operational flying began three days after the first arrival on September 14, 1970. Maintenance crews quickly "learned the ropes" on a far more advanced aircraft than their previous Canberras, and both day and night bombing practise routines were soon established. Maintainers virtually rebuilt an F-4E (A69-7234) after it was extensively damaged when an arresting wire broke during an emergency landing. One F-4E (A69-7203) was lost with its crew during a bombing sortie on the Evans Head range. The F-4E was popular with its crews, and an offer to buy the remaining 23 aircraft for $A54m as well as the F-111Cs was considered, but the type's short 25-month RAAF career ended on October 4, 1972. Most of the F-4Es were converted into F-4G Wild Weasels on return to the USA by June 1973. Six RAAF pilots had previously flown F-4C and RF-4C combat missions with USAF squadrons in Vietnam.

Egypt (Al Quwwat al Jawwiya il Misriya)

The Peace Pharaoh program transferred 35 early F-4Es, mainly from the 31st TFW, to Egypt between September 1979 and March 1980, with seven more in 1988. Following the Camp David agreement, Egypt's military aid from Arab sponsors was terminated and a US package was offered. Maintaining the F-4E proved very challenging for the Egyptian technicians, who were used to the more basic MiG-21, and availability dropped to the point where the sale of the aircraft to Turkey was contemplated in 1985. The USAF loaned a 347th TFW instructional, maintenance, and flight training team to the 222nd Fighter Regiment's Cairo West base in 1980 and supplied a similar initiative in 1983. American technicians were shocked at the poor state of the F-4Es that were returned to the USA for program depot maintenance. Egypt has since prioritized the F-16 in its defense roster and very few F-4Es remain in the inventory.

Germany (Luftwaffe)

German Phantom operations began with the RF-4E when AKG (Aufklarungsgeschwader) 51 "Immelmann" received its first aircraft in January 1971, followed by AKG52 in September 1971. Initial training began at St Louis and Shaw AFB in 1970, and an element of ground-attack instruction was added in 1988 when the aircraft were given a 5,000lb ordnance-carrying capability. Low-altitude training extended to Goose Bay, Canada from July 1980. Both units disbanded between 1993 and 1994 following the collapse of the Warsaw Pact.

When the last Luftwaffe Phantom was delivered in April 1976, F-4Fs equipped two fighter wings, each with two squadrons: JG71 "Richthofen" at Wittmund and JG74 "Molders" at Neuberg, and two bomber wings, JaBoG (Jagdbombergeschwader) 35 at Pferdsfeld and JaBoG36 at Rheine-Hopsten. The establishment of Tornado-equipped ground-attack units freed the F-4F for air defense, and the JaBoG examples were reallocated in 1990 to JG72 "Westfalen" at Hopsten and JG73 "Steinhoff." Pilots found that they lost out in close-air combat practise with MiG-29s, but they proved that the F-4F ICE's radar and AIM-120 missiles were superior to the MiG's Alamo missiles in BVR (beyond visual range) engagements. JG72 became the F-4F Flying Training Center but then disbanded in 2005, followed by JG74 in June 2008 as it completed transition to the Eurofighter under Col Uwe Klein's leadership and also completed air policing duties over the UEFA Football Championship.

Although it was commissioned in 1959, JG 71 "Richthofen" traces its origins to the beginnings of military aviation. West Germany's first interceptor wing transitioned to the F-4F from March 1974. F-4Fs 38+61 (72-1271) and 37+22 (72-1132), in the "Norm 90J" and "Norm 81B" color schemes respectively, are ICE-updated aircraft. (Author)

Many of the air forces which have operated Phantom IIs devise one-off decor for special occasions, such as the 25th anniversary of JG 74 "Molders" in September 1986. Ultramarine blue and chrome yellow paint provided this memorable effect on F-4F ICE 72-1166 37+56, destroyed in an accident on September 13, 1995. (via C. Moggeridge)

Its association with WWII ace Werner Molders was withdrawn for political reasons in 2005 but its two squadrons, 741 Staffel "Falken" and 742 Staffel "Zapata", retained their nicknames.

Within NATO the Luftwaffe was initially confined to European defense duties, but after 1994 the political situation altered to allow its squadrons to perform UN-mandated missions in other parts of the world. The F-4 was the ideal multipurpose type for these duties, exemplified when in June 2010 six Wittmund-based F-4Fs replaced USAF fighters defending Iceland at Keflavik. Phantoms from JG71 also provided Baltic Air Policing QRA (quick reaction alert) air defense in Lithuania, covering Latvia and Estonia. It was, however, the final foreign deployment for Luftwaffe F-4Fs and for JG71, the last F-4F unit, ahead of its transition to the Eurofighter after relying on the F-4 for over 38 years. The wing made its final deployment to the NATO ranges at Decimomannu, Sardinia in the summer of 2010. Twenty F-4Fs were offered to Croatia to replace that country's small MiG-21 force following a visit by F-4F 37+48 in December 2007.

JG71 was the first wing to return to Germany after training at George AFB. Two F-4Fs crewed by Oblts Rimmek and Eggert with majors Witfer and Gaede arrived at Wittmund on March 4, 1974. F-4F initial training continued at George with 12 "GA"-coded F-4Fs, later replaced by ten German-funded F-4Es. The wing had completed 50,000 F-4F flying hours by March 1980 and 250,000 hours by July 2007. At that time one of their Phantoms (37+32) had completed a record 7,000 flying hours. Excessive costs of the Eurofighter caused the retention of JG71 as the sole F-4F operator after 2008. Like JG74, it had adopted dual roles in fighter and bomber duties since the early 1980s, reverting to dedicated interception in 1988.

By 2008 training was standardized as a nine-week course at Goodyear AFB, Arizona followed by the 15-month NATO Joint Jet Pilot Training course at Sheppard AFB, Texas and the 20th FS Silver Lobos course at Holloman AFB, New Mexico. From 2005 F-4F pilot training was conducted by JG71's Ausbildungsgruppe until 2010, and pilots then took up their posts on the 15-minute QRA "Alarmrotte" roster and the NATO Immediate Reaction Force, with a dozen aircraft ready to deploy within five days. Training included in-flight refueling with Mildenhall-based USAF tankers, gunnery practise with target-towing A-4 Skyhawks, visits to the Tactical Leadership Program, and participation in other NATO fighter meets. JG71 flew a Mission Employment exercise from Mountain Home AFB, Idaho with six F-4Fs in October 2008, and it celebrated its 50th anniversary with a visit to a Maple Flag exercise in Canada by eight F-4Fs in May 2009. The squadron was scheduled to maintain a QRA at Wittmund, toting two AIM-9Ls and three external tanks until July 2013 when Eurofighters take over from its 22 F-4Fs. Training of new F-4 back-seaters ended in 2012 after the F-4F Fluglehrzentrum (OCU) disbanded at Hopsten AB in December 2005. From 2014 only the Manching test unit, WTD61, was scheduled to operate any F-4s after more than 40 years of Luftwaffe service. In 2012 a number of JG71 F-4Fs entered depot maintenance at Jever, which could enable them to remain in service for several years after the official 2014 retirement date; quite an achievement for a "stop-gap" fighter!

F-4E-39-MC 68-0444 was one of the Phantom IIs passed to Greece in November 1991 for 338 Mira, in this case with Hill Gray II colors and a USAF-style serial display. The darker gray shade weathered rapidly in the Greek climate, and was often repaired with the FS35164 blue-gray paint used on 339 Mira's interceptor F-4Es from the same 117 Wing. (Author)

Greek Air Force (Elliniki Polemiki Aeroporia)

Peace Icarus contracts provided Greece with 56 new F-4Es and eight RF-4Es in three batches between March 1974 and December 1978. Another 28 ex-USAF F-4Es were supplied in 1991. Initially, four squadrons operated Phantoms, and 117 Wing (338 "Aris" and 339 "Ajax" Miras/squadrons) at Andravida later received 38 F-4E AUP (avionics upgrade program) with updates similar to Luftwaffe F-4F ICEs. Under an EADS Peace Icarus-2000 contract they had APG-65 radars, AIM-120 missiles, new IFF equipment with four antennas above the nose, and the Rafael Litening II laser-targeting pod for LGBs. The major cockpit updates include a HUD with up-front control panel, three multi-function displays (MFDs), two of them in the rear cockpit, and a HOTAS-type throttle control. Some aircraft also have a DIAS, giving better radar warning capability and identifiable by US Navy-style antennas on the intake flanks and others below the gun and on the drag-chute door. AUP-modified aircraft, probably the most advanced Phantom IIs anywhere, emerged from Hellenic Aerospace Industry's Tanagra facility from April 1999 onward. TISEO was removed from F-4Es during AUP. 337 Mira "Fantasma" at Larissa had standard F-4Es while 348 Mira "Matia," also with Larissa's 110 Combat Wing, operated the RF-4Es, which were supplemented by 20 ex-Luftwaffe examples in 1993, with nine more to "cannibalize" for spares to sustain the force until recce-podded F-16s took over. America's need for Southern European basing agreements provided a trade-off of another 28 ex-ANG F-4Es for 338 Mira in 1991. Phantom crew training includes courses at Scholio Opion Taktikis, the Greek "Top Gun" school, with AGM-65 Maverick and AGM-130 air-to-surface missiles, keeping the aircraft current until the planned 2015 phase-out date.

Iranian Air Force (Islamic Republic of Iran Air Force)

As one of the world's largest F-4 operators during the Shah of Iran's reign, the IRIAF managed to maintain its fleet after the US trade embargo following his deposition, despite severe availability and spares problems. It was the country's principal fighter, interdictor, and interceptor during the eight-year Iran–Iraq war from September 1980. After the initial Iraqi attacks of September 22, 120 Phantoms from three bases attacked Iraqi airfields, naval, and military facilities with Mk 82 bombs and Maverick missiles, with BDA (bomb damage assessment) follow-up by RF-4Es. In later engagements losses were heavy, though many F-4s took severe SAM and AAA damage from Iraq's massive, multilayered defenses but returned safely. Their evasion tactics mirrored those of USAF pilots over North Vietnam who had faced the same weapons, but Iraq's were even more numerous and ECM pods weren't available until later in the conflict. Iraqi ships were sunk with Mavericks, but several F-4s were ambushed and shot down by Iraqi Mirages and MiG-25s. On deep penetration missions, F-4s struck the massive western Iraq H-3 airfield, petrochemical facilities, and the Tamuz nuclear plant near Baghdad. AVQ-9 "Zot" Pave Light GBU-10 LGB (laser-guided bomb) strikes were made on bridges and oil facilities by F-4Ds. F-4 pilots, some flying over 1,000 combat sorties, claimed more than 80 Iraqi MiG, Mirage, and Exocet-carrying Super Etendard aircraft destroyed, mainly with AIM-9P and AIM-7E-2 missiles. They repelled a determined land invasion by Saddam Hussein's forces. Fighting on a reduced scale continued for six years until a last, desperate attempt to stop a second Iraqi invasion ended in the July 19, 1988 ceasefire.

In 2009 the possibility of Israeli attacks on Iran's nuclear research facilities prompted the refurbishing of a number of stored aircraft including F-4D/E Phantoms. Modifications included radar and avionics updates and compatibility with the Russian Kh-58/AS-11 Kilter antiradiation missile, the Iranian Kite-2000 CBU dispenser, and Chinese C-802K-2 antishipping missiles. The original AIM-7 and AIM-9P air-to-air armament was retained rather than Russian AA-10 Alamo and AA-11 Archer missiles (which were tested), and some F-4Es were adapted as in-flight refuelers, using Beech 1800 pods and extra drop tanks. This restored F-4 strength to around 64 F-4Es in six squadrons at Nojeh, Bushehr, and Bandar Abbas airbases out of the probable 32 F-4Ds, 177 F-4Es, and 17 RF-4Es in 12 squadrons delivered between September 1968 and August 1979. About 12 F-4D interceptors and nine RF-4Es also remained in 2011.

Israeli Defence Forces/Air Force (ADF/AF, Heyl Ha'Avir)

Israel first approached the USA concerning F-4 Kurnass (Sledge Hammer) deliveries in 1965 but permission wasn't given until 1968, followed by an order for 44 hard-wing F-4Es with optical gun sights, AIM-9 (rather than AIM-4) missiles, and no nuclear capability or TISEO. Training began in the USA in 1969 just before the War of Attrition with Egypt, and Peace Echo 1 F-4Es began to arrive for 201 Sqn by September 1969. Further Peace Echo/ Peace Patch deliveries took the F-4E total to around 215 by November 1976. The Phantoms were in action from October 9 over the disputed Suez Canal region, claiming their first MiG-21 on November 11, 1969 with an AIM-9B and losing the first Kurnass to Egypt's heavy Soviet-managed SAM and AAA defenses on November 17 during one of many defense-suppression missions flown at the time. The F-4E enabled unprecedented deep-penetration strikes into Egypt, combining heavy bomb-loads with effective self-defense armament to defeat MiGs. The "Pricha" (Orange Blossom) attacks by Kurnass flights on a SAM training center and Egyptian commando HQ in January 1970 capitalized on this strength. Shipping attacks, night interdiction, and frequent clashes with MiGs (although Mirages still took most of the air-to-air missions) continued through 1970, though the increasing Soviet SA-2 and SA-3 missile batteries took a heavy toll. US-supplied AN/ALQ-87 ECM pods initially proved ineffective against coordinated SAM launches, causing five Kurnass losses in a month. Antiradiation Shrike missiles were supplied, also stand-off Walleye and HOBOS missiles, and these were also used against Syrian SAM batteries.

AIM-9D Sidewinders ("Dekers"), used from May 1970, increased the MiG-kill ratio, and Kurnass losses ended during a comparative lull between August 1970 and October 6, 1973, when simultaneous Egyptian and Syrian surprise attacks signaled the start of the Yom Kippur War. However, Syria's SAM network had received massive Soviet improvement, and seven F-4Es were destroyed on October 7 SEAD missions. Kurnass missions by whole squadrons of F-4Es against air defenses, troop concentrations, and "hardened" airfields cost at least 37 F-4Es that month, often due to inadequate information on the location of defenses, including the new SA-6 Gainful missile. By October 24, when a cease-fire was observed, Israel had regained ascendency, although for the first time its air force was unable to gain air superiority without army participation despite the urgent transfer of up to 40 USAF F-4Es as attrition replacements in mid-October.

Postwar, the air defense missions steadily passed to the new F-15A Eagles, which rapidly devastated Syria's fighters in combat, achieving an 85:0 kill rate in the 1978–82 Lebanon conflict. The five Kurnass squadrons, progressively upgraded with TISEO, AN/ALE-40 chaff/flare dispensers, external refueling probes, and leading edge slats, continued to fly LGB and SEAD missions in ongoing skirmishes over Egypt and intense action in the Lebanon, destroying Syria's SAM network without loss. Their value as ground-attackers and their overall versatility became increasingly appreciated by pilots. They flew long-range interdictions, killing MiGs on the return flight and using their impressive acceleration to climb out of trouble, something that no other IDF/AF aircraft could equal. Kurnass units were originally slated to attack Iraq's Osirak nuclear reactor (Operation *Opera*), but the newly introduced GD F-16 fighters could fly the mission without tankers. On June 11, 1982, Ben-Ami Peri and David Oakman shot down a MiG-21, the 116th and final Kurnass victory. New weapons, the GBU-15 LGB, long-range Delilah and AGM-142 Popeye missiles, and Python 3 air-to-air missile, had been introduced from 1977 onwards, and the Kurnass 2000 was first used over Lebanon on February 5, 1992. From 1994, 69 Squadron "Hammers" was the first Kurnass unit to wind down and prepare for the F-15I Ra'am (a Strike Eagle derivative) and F-16I Sufa, which gradually replaced the F-4 between 2004 and 2008.

A 1968 order for six RF-4E (Kurnass Tsilum) was not delivered until February 1971, so training was conducted using two Israeli-marked 10th TRW, USAFE RF-4Cs from August 1970 at Ramat David air base and two F-4Es temporarily converted to carry a KS-87 camera in their gun-bays in

The F-4's J79 is still considered to be one of the world's most reliable turbojets, and its 17,900lb of afterburning power was key to the aircraft's success. However, some former single-seat pilots tended to find the Phantom's weight and 1950s aerodynamics made it quite "draggy": "close the throttles and it will just stop" was one reaction, while another former Mirage pilot compared the F-4 to a "twin turbocharged Mack truck." Two fighter generations later, the F-119-PW-100s of the F-22A Raptor deliver twice the power for a slightly heavier airframe than a loaded F-4 and offer Mach 1.7 speed without afterburner, while the F135, for the F-35 Lightning II, will generate up to 50,000lb thrust from a single powerplant. (Author)

place of the Vulcan cannon. They flew with 119 Sqn during the Yom Kippur War, relying on speed to evade Russian-operated MiG-25s but losing one RF-4E (number 194) to a barrage of 11 SA-2 SAMs on November 9, 1973 and another when a flare caused an internal fire. Six more RF-4Es with AN/APD-10 SLAR and AN/UPD-4 datalink were delivered from 1977, and three Peace Jack F-4E conversions. RF-4E crews wore David Clark pressurized "space suits" on missions above 50,000ft.

F-4EJ Kai 67-8379 in one of the color scheme variations it wore with 305 Hikotai, one of the five JASDF with which units it served. It was one of the last Phantom IIs with 306 Hikotai in 1996, and represented 8 Hikotai at the 1998 JASDF Fighter Meet, but was lost in an accident later that year. (Author's collection)

Japan (Japan Air Self-Defense Force)

With 140 F-4EJ and 14 RF-4E Phantoms acquired since 1971, the JASDF maintained four Phantom units between 1994 and 2009 out of seven originally commissioned. The 303rd Hikotai (formed in 1976) and 304th (1977), 305th (1978), and 306th (1997) Hikotais were air-defense exponents, converting to the F-15J Eagle between 1989 and 1997. At Naha, Okinawa, the 302nd Hikotai (originally based at Chitose from October 1974) stayed with the F-4EJ Kai decorated with an Ojiro Washi eagle insignia. This squadron moved again to Hayakuri in March 2009. Komatsu air base housed the 306th Hikotai, the first to receive the F-4EJ Kai in August 1989. A later unit, the 8th Hikotai at Misawa AB, received the 306th Hikotai's F-4EJs to replace its Mitsubishi F1s from 1995 in antishipping and air-to-surface roles. At Hayakuri the 501st Hikotai flew the dwindling numbers of green-and-tan-camouflaged reconnaissance RF-4E/EJs from 1974, while the 301st Hikotai at Nyutabaru was the first F-4EJ unit in October 1973 and continued as an operational conversion/air defense unit from 1973. The Misawa unit, famous for its glorious blue-themed color schemes, transitioned to the Mitsubishi F2 by March 2009. Some of its pilots had been flying the Phantom for up to 25 years.

JASDF Phantoms maintain a constant air-defense alert, often intercepting Chinese and Russian aircraft probing the country's defenses. Reconnaissance around Japan's extensive coastline was performed in 2012 by around ten remaining woodpecker-decorated RF-4Es and surplus RF-4EJ Kais, the latter using three different sensor pods including the Thomson-CSF TACER electronic surveillance pod to offer similar coverage to the RF-4E. In 2011 Japan chose to replace its Phantoms with 42 F-35A Lighting IIs from 2016, though some F-4s may remain in service until 2017.

EGYPT, OCTOBER 1973

Senior pilot Asher Snir and Aharon Katz of No 119 "Bat" Squadron Israeli Defense Force/Air Force were flying as "Secretary 1," leading a bombing attack on Tanta air base, Egypt on October 15, 1973. The bomb-load from their Kurnass (No. 119) was delivered successfully, but they were approached by two Egyptian AF MiG-21MFs close to the target. Snir engaged afterburner and maneuvered behind one of the MiGs that was pursuing his F-4E wingman. Using cannon to avoid the risk of a missile hitting his wingman, ace pilot Snir fired a burst of 20mm and the MiG disintegrated. Avoiding missiles from a second MiG, he escaped at low altitude.

F-4D-29-MC 66-7479 was among the Peace Pheasant Phantom IIs delivered to South Korea in November 1990 for the 11th TFW at Daegu, where this aircraft is landing. Visibility over the nose for landing was poor and many pilots cranked the seat up to see better at that time. The side view was restricted by high canopy rails, particularly in the back cockpit, and the pilot had to roll slightly to see much laterally. (Author's collection)

Spain's RF-4Cs outlived its F-4Cs in squadron service, surviving until 2002. Ala de Casa 12, with both types, was part of a five-squadron USAFE/Spanish Phantom force at Torrejon until Spain evicted all US military units in 1983. CR12-58 was RF-4C-26-MC 65-0897, delivered from ANG stocks in 1995 and finally used as a "parts locker" before disposal at the Bardenas Reales range. (Author's collection)

Republic of Korea Air Force (Hankook Kong Goon)

Eighteen F-4Ds were ordered in 1968 during a period of tension between North and South Korea that included the seizure of the US ship *Pueblo*, and they arrived from August 1969. Thirty more were supplied under various loan or purchase arrangements by 1988, and 37 new-built Peace Pheasant F-4Es followed by 1978 for the 17th Fighter Wing at Cheongjiu. Another 30 were supplied in 1989, and additions have subsequently taken the total to 92 F-4Ds and 103 F-4Es, some equipped with Pave Spike and Pave Tack target designating pods and Popeye missile capability. Twenty-seven RF-4Cs and a number of AN/ALQ-131 jamming pods were delivered from 1988 for the 131st TRS at Suwon. The surviving F-4Ds equipped the 110th and 151st TFS at Daegu until Boeing F-15Ks took over their role and the F-4Es at Cheongju flew with the 152nd, 153rd, and 156th TFS. Like other F-4 customers, the Koreans evaluated SLEP programs, including a proposal from DASA in Germany to upgrade its F-4Es with ICE-pattern avionics, but the cost of the F-15K purchase has ruled out all but the most basic airframe life enhancements.

Spanish Air Force (Ejercito del Aire)

F-4C-24-MC 64-820 (Spanish serial C.12-37) of Ala 12 (12 Wing) flew the last Spanish AF F-4C sortie on September 13, 1990, closing out a service record that began on June 17, 1971. The Peace Alpha program provided 36 F-4C(S) Phantoms and three Boeing KC-97L refuelers in return for continued USAF use of Spain's Zaragoza and Torrejon air bases. The F-4Cs (dubbed "flying wardrobes") derived mainly from the USAFE 81st TFW as it converted to the F-4D, with four 1978 attrition replacements from the 58th TFTW. All were overhauled at CASA-Getafe, where USAFE F-4s had passed through PDM since 1967. Ala 12's two squadrons, the 121st and 122nd escuadrons, took 18 Phantoms each, while the KC-97Ls went to the 123rd Esc, where they were replaced in 1976 by KC-130Hs. Maintenance of the well-worn F-4Cs was assisted by the Torrejon-based 401st TFW, USAFE, and Ala 12 became operational in 1973. Joint exercises with Spanish and Portuguese units as well as USAF and US Navy forces followed to vary their basic task of air defense. After Spain fully joined NATO in 1982, F-4s were involved in many exchanges and exercises. AIM-9B missiles were replaced by AIM-9Js in 1978 and SUU-16/A gun-pods were also supplied, together with surplus AN/ALQ-72 ECM pods and some GBU-10 LGBS. Air combat practise was provided by Spanish Mirage units and 401st TFW F-4Es and F-16s. Diminishing numbers and spares shortages caused the steady withdrawal of the F-4Cs from 1985 and replacement by EF-18A/B Hornets.

Four ex-363rd TRW RF-4Cs were also received in 1978 for 122 Esc, used mainly for civilian surveillance contracts. Another 14 ex-ANG RF-4Cs were also acquired by 1995. Transferred to the reactivated 123 Escuadron,

these more recently updated RF-4Cs were fitted with Israeli-designed fixed in-flight refueling probes (to handle the KC-130H drogue refueling system when the "flying boom" KC-97Ls were retired in 1976) and AN/APQ-172 radars. They continued in service until May 28, 2002.

Turkish Air Force (Turk Hava Kuvvetleri – THK)

Turkey's first two F-4Es were delivered under Peace Diamond III on August 30, 1974, and by 1992 the country had received 237 F-4Es and RF-4Es, many of which were still in service after almost 40 years. The USA delivered the final 40 F-4Es in gratitude for the use of Turkey's Incirlik AB during Operation *Desert Storm*. One RF-4E and seven F-4E squadrons were then operational. In 2009 Turkey undertook an RF-4ETM upgrade program, Project Isik (Light) for up to 20 ex-Luftwaffe aircraft that were then consolidated into a single unit, 113 Filo "Isik" at Eskisehir. They received a new multi-function display, datalink and other systems developed for the F-4E-2020. Fifty-four F-4Es were upgraded as F-4E 2020 Terminators by Israel Aircraft Industries and the THK from 1999 to approximate Kurnass 2000 specification but with Elta EL/M-2032 radars, and another 48 conversions were planned, keeping the aircraft potentially viable until 2020.

Erhac-based 172 Filo was disbanded in 2009 after more than 30 Phantom years, awaiting reequipment with the F-35 in 2014, leaving 132/111 Filo with F-4E-2020s. Later armament additions included the Nufuz Edici Bomba (NEB), an 870kg, dual-warhead bunker-buster, and the KGK-82 "smart" glide-bomb, based on the Mk 82 munition. Training took place on Turkey's air combat maneuvering instrumentation (ACMI) range at Konya, where F-4 crews often flew against fighters from Pakistan, Holland, the USA, and Italy.

CONCLUSION

Launched into battle within a year of the first USAF wing achieving operational readiness, the F-4C's virtues and drawbacks were soon revealed. In air-to-air combat, "with no gun and missiles whose reliability was about 10 percent you'd have to rate it low," in MiG-killer Ralph Wetterhahn's estimation.

> The only real advantage we had was to accelerate out of a fight. I'd trade that for turn performance. Turning with a MiG-17 was suicide. You could do pretty well turning with a MiG-21, but he was so small it was tough to keep him in sight. We were twice the size of the MiGs and had that big smoke-trail. Still, I'd take that ride into Hanoi over the F-105 Thunderchief any day.

The Phantom II's versatility was always a major strength, although politicians initially sought to over-emphasize that characteristic. Ralph Wetterhahn recalled "Rapid Roger," a 1966 "sortie generation" exercise that he thought was

> an idiotic attempt to fully utilize each F-4 both day and night. Maintenance did a circus act downloading the night configuration (centerline tank and outboard wing pylons with flares and bombs) and uploading the day stuff (wing tanks, centerline MER, missiles). A lot of guys died because of that nutty attempt by McNamara's minions to "maximize utilization."

F-4E-33-MC 66-0361 was one of 40 Peace Diamond V aircraft for the Turkish AF. It was recovered from AMARC in 1986 for 3ci Ana Jet Us, 2nd Tactical Air Force at Konya AB. F-4 canopies were made of acrylic plastic, opening to 53 degrees. Each has an emergency jettison system using air compressed at 3000psi. Canopies had to be closed above 60mph but were left open for taxiing in hot conditions, as the air conditioning didn't operate until the Phantom was airborne. (Author's collection)

Phantoms in that war became the most important tactical aircraft, performing diverse tasks ranging from Fast FAC (forward air control) to flare dropping or, on one occasion, delivering a Fulton Recovery System apparatus to a downed pilot. They dropped Igloo White sensors on the Ho Chi Minh Trail, laser-guided bombs on Hanoi's bridges, and propaganda leaflets everywhere.

In later conflicts, land-based F-4s responded with deadly effect in scenarios including the eight-year Iran–Iraq War, where Phantom crews claimed 80 aerial kills during low-altitude attacks that destroyed a substantial proportion of Saddam Hussein's forces. Forty years after Vietnam, digitally "re-lifed" F-4s are still "turning and burning" with the best modern fighters in several air forces, flown by a generation of pilots born after the Phantom left front-line US service. The F-4 gave many nations their first experience of multirole, supersonic tactical air power with a machine that has outlasted most of their previous equipment.

Its successor at St Louis, the F-15 Eagle, was taking shape on McDonnell's drawing boards by 1967 and it took the F-4 concept many stages further, with more power (allowing acceleration in vertical flight), much improved visibility, a gun, and far greater maneuverability. The F-15C's 100:0 kill-to-loss ratio in combat has proved its superb qualities as a pure fighter, and its F-15E derivative vastly extended the capability of the two-seat strike fighter concept pioneered by F-4 crews. Another generation on from the Eagle, the Lockheed-Martin F-22A Raptor combined stealth characteristics with even more spectacular performance, although in both F-15 and F-22 dedicated tactical reconnaissance versions like the RF-4 series were dropped. The Raptor's F-119-PW-100s deliver twice the J79's power in a slightly heavier airframe than a loaded F-4 and offer Mach 1.7 speed without afterburner, while the F135 engine for the F-35 Lightning II fighter generates up to 50,000lb thrust from a single powerplant. Dedicating an F-4 memorial to a MiG killer, Col Larry Golberg, USAF director of History and Museums (and Vietnam F-4 veteran) Dick Anderegg commented that the F-4 was "proof positive that if you put enough thrust behind a brick you can make it fly. It's a brute but the power and magnificence of this machine were a joy, always."

FURTHER READING

Aloni, Shlomo, *Arab–Israeli Air Wars 1947–82*, Osprey Publishing (2001)

Aloni, Shlomo, *Israeli F-4 Phantom II Aces*, Osprey Publishing (2004)

Anderegg, C. R., *Sierra Hotel, Flying Air Force Fighters in the Decade after Vietnam*, Ross & Perry (2001)

Bishop, Farzad, and Cooper, Tom, *Iranian F-4 Phantom II Units in Combat*, Osprey Publishing (2003)

Bugos, Glenn E., *Engineering the F-4 Phantom II – Parts into Systems*, Naval Institute Press (1996)

Cohen, Eliezer, Col, *Israel's Best Defense*, Crown Publishers (1993)

Davies, Peter E., *USAF F-4 Phantom II MiG Killers 1965–68*, Osprey Publishing (2004)

Davies, Peter E., *USAF F-4 Phantom II MiG Killers 1972–73*, Osprey Publishing (2005)

Davies, Peter E., *F-4 Phantom II vs MiG-21 – USAF & VPAF in the Vietnam War*, Osprey Publishing (2008)

Dimitropoulos, Kostas, *F-4 Phantom*, Constantinidis Publications (1997)

Eisel, Brick, and Schreiner, Jim, *Magnum! The Wild Weasels in Desert Storm*, Pen & Sword (2009)

Fearis, Peter, *Defenders of Nippon: F-4 Phantom II*, Kaburaya Books (2002)

Francillon, Rene, *McDonnell F-4D*, Aerofax, Inc. (1985)

Gunston, Bill, *The Development of Jet and Turbine Aero Engines*, PSL (1995)

Harty, John J., *The Business History of the F-4 Program*, McDonnell Aircraft Company (1990)

Harty, John J., *F-4 Phantom II Program Milestones*, McDonnell Aircraft Company (1988)

Jahnke, Ralf, *McDonnell-Douglas RF-4E Phantom* II, F40 P.ecom (2000)

Johnson, Val Ross, *Night Owl Fighter Pilot*, Universe (2006)

Logan, Don, *The 388th Tactical Fighter Wing*, Schiffer Military History (1995)

McCarthy, Mike, *Phantom Reflections*, Praeger Security International (2007)

McDonnell Aircraft Company, *F-4 Program History* (1992)

McGovern, Tim, *McDonnell F-4E Phantom II*, Aerofax, Inc. (1987)

Melampy, Jake, *The Modern Phantom Guide*, Reid Air Publications (2009)

Mersky, Peter B., *Israeli Fighter Aces*, Specialty Press Publishers (1997)

Miller, Jay, *McDonnell RF-4 Variants*, Aerofax, Inc. (1984)

Momyer, William W., *Airpower in Three Wars*, University Press of the Pacific (2002)

Nordeen, Lon, *Fighters Over Israel*, Greenhill Books (1990)

O'Brien, Frank J., *The Hungry Tigers – the Fighter Pilot's Role in Modern Warfare*, TAB Books (1986)

Olds, Robin (with Christina Olds and Ed Rasimus), *Fighter Pilot*, St Martin's Press (2010)

Peake, William R., *F-4 Phantom II Production and Operational Data*, Midland Publishing (2004)

Rasimus, Ed, *Palace Cobra*, St Martin's Press (2006)

Riedel, Jay E., *Memories of a Fighter Pilot*, Lulu.com (2003)

Ross, Bob, *The Warriors*, Yucca Free Press (2002)

Thornborough, Anthony, and Davies, Peter E., *The Phantom Story*, Cassell & Co. (2000)

Wilson, Stewart, *Phantom, Hornet and Skyhawk in Australian Service*, Aerospace Publications (1993)

Documents

Wogstad, James (ed.), *US Nuclear Bombs*, Replica in Scale 3/3 (1976)

Wogstad, James, and Fridell, Phil, *American Aircraft Bombs 1917-1974*, Replica in Scale 2/3 (1974)

TO 1F-4G-1 *F-4G Flight Manual*, Secretary of the Air Force (1978)

TO 1F-4G-34-1-1 *F-4G Aircrew Weapons Delivery Manual*, Secretary of the Air Force (1978)

TO 1F-4(R)-C-1 *RF-4C Flight Manual*, Secretary of the Air Force (1972)

TO 1F-4C-3-1-1 *USAF F-4 Structural Repair, Organizational and Field Manual*, Secretary of the Air Force (1971) P.S. 111 *F/RF-4C Crew Chief's Handbook*, McDonnell Aircraft Co. (1965)

INDEX